SCARY READERS THEATRE

SCARY READERS THEATRE

Suzanne I. Barchers

TEACHER IDEAS PRESS
A Division of
Libraries Unlimited, Inc.
Englewood, Colorado
1994

For Norma Olson,
whose courage is inspirational

TEACHER IDEAS PRESS
A Division of
Libraries Unlimited, Inc.
P.O. Box 6633
Englewood, CO 80155-6633
1-800-237-6124

Project Editor: Tama J. Serfoss
Copy Editor: Tama J. Serfoss
Proofreader: Suzanne H. Burke
Design and Layout: Pamela J. Getchell

Library of Congress Cataloging-in-Publication Data

Barchers, Suzanne I.
    Scary readers theatre / Suzanne I. Barchers.
    xiii, 157 p. 22x28 cm.
    Includes bibliographical references and index.
    ISBN 1-56308-292-6
    1. Folklore and children.   2. Folklore and education.
  3. Folklore--Study and teaching (Elementary)   I. Title.
  GR43.C4B37   1994
  808.5'45--dc20   94-31715
                                                    CIP

Contents

PART 3

PART 4

ACKNOWLEDGMENTS

"Aaron Kelly's Bones" was adapted from *Scary Stories to Tell in the Dark*, collected by Alvin Schwartz, J. B. Lippincott, 1981. Copyright © 1981 Alvin Schwartz. Reprinted by permission of HarperCollins Publishers.

"Antoine" was adapted from "The Story of a Very Bad Boy"; "The Punishment" was adapted from "The Jogi's Punishment"; and "The Thieving Lad" was adapted from "The Shifty Lad" in *The Lilac Fairy Book*, edited by Andrew Lang, Dover Publications, 1968.

"The Black Cats Are Talking" and "The Tale of the Talking Eggs" were adapted from *Great American Folklore: Tales, Ballads and Superstitions from All Across America*, compiled by Kemp P. Battle, Barnes and Noble Books, 1986.

"Bolster," "Fowler's Fowl," "Janet and Tam Lin," "Rachel's Curse," "The Robber Bridegroom," and "The Witches with the Horns" were adapted from *Wise Women: Folk and Fairy Tales from around the World*, retold and edited by Suzanne I. Barchers, Libraries Unlimited, 1990.

"Brave Heart" was adapted from "The Evil Old Witch" in *Great Myths and Legends: The 1984 Childcraft Annual*, World Book, Inc., 1984.

"The Fiddler's Contest" was adapted from "Fiddler's Dram" in *God Bless the Devil! Bench Tales*, edited by James R. Aswell, Julia Willhoit, Jennette Edwards, E. E. Miller, and Lena Lipscomb. Copyright © 1940 by the University of North Carolina Press.

"Jack and His Master" was adapted from *Celtic Fairy Tales*, collected by Joseph Jacobs, Dover Publications, 1968.

"The Thief and the Liar" was adapted from "The Partnership of the Thief and the Liar" in *The Grey Fairy Book*, edited by Andrew Lang, Dover Publications, 1967.

"The Tinderbox" and "The Wolf and the Seven Little Kids" were excerpted from *Readers Theatre for Beginning Readers*, by Suzanne I. Barchers, Teacher Ideas Press, 1993.

"The Voice of Death" was adapted from *The Red Fairy Book*, edited by Andrew Lang, Dover Publications, 1966.

Introduction

NOT FOR THE FAINT OF HEART

The scripts in this collection were chosen because they are a bit mischievous, ghostly, monstrous, or downright frightening. Drawn from Greek myths, folk tales, ghost stories, and modern urban legends, they provide teachers with an enticing collection of deliciously scary stories from around the world. Peopled by witches, trolls, ghosts, monsters, robbers, and tricksters, these tales will be recognized by many students because they are adapted from familiar sources.

THE ROLE OF READERS THEATRE

Readers theatre is a presentation by two or more participants who read from scripts and interpret a literary work in such a way that the audience imaginatively senses characterization, setting, and action. Voice and body tension rather than movement are involved, thus eliminating the need for the many practice sessions that timing and action techniques require in the presentation of a play (Laughlin and Latrobe 1990, 3).

Traditionally, the primary focus of readers theatre is on an effective reading of the script rather than on a dramatic, memorized presentation. Because many of the scripts are familiar, students will naturally paraphrase their reading, an acceptable practice. Generally, there are minimal props and movement on the stage, although adding such touches enlivens the production and invites more active participation, especially with primary students.

The ease of incorporating readers theatre into the language arts program offers teachers an exciting way to enhance the program, particularly in today's classrooms that emphasize a variety of reading and listening experiences. All scripts were evaluated with the Flesch-Kincaid Readability Scale and are grouped into sections of second-, third-, fourth-, or fifth-grade readability levels (parts 1, 2, 3, and 4, respectively). Before using, each script should be further evaluated by the teacher for content or vocabulary that might be challenging to students.

The performance of readers theatre scripts also encourages strong oral skills for readers and promotes active listening for students in the audience (Sloyer 1982, 4). Students explore literature in a new form, and the class can begin to analyze various treatments of the same or similar stories by comparing these to versions they have heard or read. Additional benefits are the pleasure of performing for parents or other classes and the ease of preparing for special days when a program is expected.

PREPARING THE SCRIPTS

Once a script is chosen for reading, make a copy for each character, plus an extra set or two for your own use and a replacement copy. To help beginning or remedial readers keep their place on the page, use highlighter markers to designate a character's name within the copy. For example, in any given story, the role of the narrator could be highlighted in blue each time it appears, with other parts highlighted in different colors. This helps readers track their parts and eases management of scripts in the event pages become mixed. Line numbers are included in the right margin for easy prompting by the teacher to a specific line.

Photocopied scripts will last longer if you use a three-hole punch (or copy them on prepunched paper) and place them in inexpensive folders. The folders can be color coordinated to the internal highlighting for each character's part. The title of the play can be printed on the outside of the folder, and scripts can be stored easily for the next reading. Preparing the scripts and folders is a good task for a volunteer parent or an older student helper. The preparation takes a minimum of initial attention and needs to be repeated only when a folder is lost.

GETTING STARTED

For the first experience with a readers theatre script, choose one with many characters to involve as many students as possible. Gather the students informally, perhaps in a circle on the floor. If a story or picture book version of the chosen script is available, read it aloud to the students. Then introduce the script version and explain that readers theatre does not mean memorizing a play and acting it out, but rather reading a script aloud with perhaps a few props and actions. Select volunteers to do the initial reading, allowing them an opportunity to review their parts before reading aloud. Other students could examine other versions, brainstorm prop ideas, or preview other scripts.

Before reading the first script, decide whether to choose parts after the reading or to introduce additional scripts to involve more students. A readers theatre workshop could be held periodically, with every student belonging to a group that prepares a script for presentation. A readers theatre festival could be planned for a special day when several short scripts are presented consecutively, with brief intermissions between each reading. Groups of tales could include the well-known Grimm tales, those drawn from mythology, tales of trickery, or tales from specific countries. Consider these groupings drawn from this collection:

Ghosts and Fairies: "The Fiddler's Contest," "The Headless Haunt," "Janet and Tam Lin," and "Aaron Kelly's Bones."

Grave stories: "The Grave," "The Girl with the Lavender Dress," "The Fiddler's Contest," "The Headless Haunt," and "Aaron Kelly's Bones."

Witch stories: "Brave Heart" and "The Witches with the Horns."

Heads: "The Headless Haunt," "The Red Ribbon," " The Tale of the Talking Eggs," and "The Hydra."

Retribution: "Rachel's Curse" and "The Punishment."

Once the students have read the scripts and become familiar with new vocabulary, determine which students will read the various parts. In assigning roles, strive for a balance between males and females. Some roles are animals or characters that could be read by either sex. Some parts are considerably more demanding than others, and students should be encouraged to volunteer for roles that they will be comfortable reading. Once they are familiar with readers theatre, students should be encouraged to stretch and try reading a role that is challenging for them. Though one goal for incorporating readers theatre into the curriculum is to develop and inspire competent readers, it is equally important that the students succeed and enjoy the literature.

PRESENTATION SUGGESTIONS

For readers theatre, readers traditionally stand—or sit on stools, chairs, or the floor—in an informal presentation style. The narrator may stand slightly off to one side with the script placed on a music stand or lectern. The readers may hold their scripts in folders.

The position of the reader indicates the importance of the role. For example, Rachel in "Rachel's Curse" would have a position in the front center of the stage, with the minor characters to the sides and slightly behind her. In "The Fiddler's Contest," the narrator, county clerk, Coot, and Ples could be on one side of the stage with the other characters entering and remaining on the other side of the stage for their lines.

Because these scripts are appropriate for developing and remedial readers, it is important that the students are comfortable with the physical arrangement. It is assumed that the students will present informally, perhaps adapting or enlivening the traditional readers theatre style. Therefore, a traditional arrangement for presenters is not provided with the scripts. Instead, a few general suggestions are supplied for each play. For example, readers of brief parts may enter or leave the stage prior to and following their parts. Alternatively, readers may stand up for a reading and sit down for the remainder of the script.

Determining the presentation arrangement is a good cooperative activity for the readers. The arrangement should foster success; students who cannot stand quietly for a long period of time should be allowed to sit on a chair, a pillow, or the floor. Restless students with a short reading could remain on stage only for the duration of the reading. However, students may have fresh ideas for a different presentation, and their involvement should be fostered.

PROPS

Readers theatre traditionally has no, or few, props. However, simple costuming effects, such as a hat, apron, or scarf, plus a few props on stage will lend interest to the presentation. Shirlee Sloyer (1982, 58) suggests that a script can become a property: "a book, a fan, a gun, or any other object mentioned in the story." Suggestions for simple props or costuming are included; however, students should be encouraged to decide how much or little to add to their production. The use of props or actions may be overwhelming for some readers, and the emphasis should remain on the reading, rather than on an overly complicated presentation.

DELIVERY

In an effort to keep the scripts easy for readers, few delivery suggestions are written within the scripts. Therefore, it is important to discuss with the students what will make the scripts come alive as they read. Primary students naturally incorporate voices into their creative play and should be encouraged to explore how this same practice will enhance their reading. Small groups working on individual plays should be invited to brainstorm various delivery styles. A variety of warm-ups can help students with expression. For example, have the entire class respond to the following situations that have similar themes as those in this collection:

- discovering a snake has gotten loose

- suspecting a monster is under your bed

- learning you have been tricked

- having someone jump out of the closet at you

- discovering your best friend is a ghost

- having witches take over your house

- discovering your cat can talk

- having a genie or fairy appear with three wishes

At first, it is tempting for students to keep their heads buried in the script, making sure they don't miss a line. Students should learn the material well enough to be able to look up during a presentation. Students can learn to use onstage focus, where they focus on each other during the presentation. This is most logical for characters who are interacting with each other. The use of offstage focus, where the presenters look directly into the eyes of the audience, is more logical for the narrator or characters who are uninvolved with onstage characters. An alternative is to have students who do not interact with each other focus on a prearranged offstage location, such as the classroom clock, during delivery.

Simple actions can also be incorporated into readers theatre. Though primary students are generally less inhibited than older students, encourage readers to use action by practicing panto-mime in groups. If possible, have a mime come for a presentation and some introductory instruction. Alternatively, introduce mime by having students act out the following familiar actions: combing hair, brushing teeth, turning the pages of a book, eating an ice cream cone, making a phone call, and falling asleep. Then select and try general activities drawn from the scripts: rocking, waving, jumping, fiddling, and so forth. These actions need not be elaborate; characters can indicate falling asleep simply by closing their eyes. Although readers theatre uses minimal gestures and actions, using them can brighten a presentation for both participants and audience.

Generally, the audience should be able to see the readers' facial expressions during the reading. Upon occasion a script lends itself to a character moving across the stage, facing another character while reading. In this event, the presenters should be turned enough that the audience can see their faces.

The use of music can enhance the delivery of the play. For "The Fiddlers Contest" or "Aaron Kelly's Bones," use violin music during parts of the play. Royal music may accompany the kings' roles in "The Thief and the Liar." Signals could foreshadow disaster, such as a drum beat just before the narrator tells that the wife's head has fallen off in "The Red Ribbon." As with props and action, music should be used sparingly, as the emphasis should remain on the reading.

THE AUDIENCE

When students are part of the audience, they should understand their role. Caroline Feller Bauer (1990, 30) recommends that students rehearse applauding and reacting appropriately to the script. Challenge the students to determine if the audience might provide sound effects, such as joining in with the hobyahs' chant in "The Hobyahs." Cue cards that prompt the audience to make noises can be incorporated into the production. Encourage students to find additional ways to involve the audience in the program.

BEYOND SCARY READERS THEATRE

Once students have enjoyed the reading process involved in preparing and presenting readers theatre, the next logical step is to involve them in the writing process of creating their own scripts. Consult your librarian for sources of more scary stories. The options for readers theatre scripts are endless, and students will naturally want to translate a favorite story into a script. For an in-depth discussion of this process, consult part 1 of Shirlee Sloyer's *Readers Theatre: Story Dramatization in the Classroom*.

REFERENCES

Bauer, Caroline Feller. *Read for the Fun of It: Active Programming with Books for Children.* Illustrated by Lynn Gates Bredeson. Bronx, NY: H. W. Wilson, 1992.

Laughlin, Mildred Knight, and Kathy Howard Latrobe. *Readers Theatre for Children: Scripts and Script Development.* Englewood, CO: Teacher Ideas Press, 1990.

Sloyer, Shirlee. *Readers Theatre: Story Dramatization in the Classroom.* Urbana, IL: National Council of Teachers of English, 1982.

Part I

The Black Cats Are Talking

The Black Cats Are Talking

SUMMARY

In this American tale, a woodcutter is coming home when he meets nine black cats carrying a dead cat on a stretcher. The cats ask him to tell Aunt Kan that Polly Grundy is dead. He shares the story with his wife, with unexpected results.
Reading level: 2.

PRESENTATION SUGGESTIONS

The main characters, the narrator and the woodcutter, should have the central focus. The black cats could be to one side of them, with the wife and yellow cat on the other side.

PROPS

Students could bring in a variety of stuffed toy cats or make cutouts of black cats to be propped around the stage. Consider adding props or drawings to depict the fire or dinnertime.

CHARACTERS

Narrator

Woodcutter

First Cat

Second Cat

Wife

Yellow Cat

From *Scary Readers Theatre.* © 1994 Suzanne I. Barchers. Teacher Ideas Press. P.O. Box 6633, Englewood, CO 80155. 1-800-237-6124.

The Black Cats Are Talking

Narrator:
Once there was an old man who was a woodcutter. One night he was coming home from his work. He was looking forward to his supper and a warm fire. Suddenly, he saw a passle of black cats in the road.

1

Woodcutter:
Look at that mess of cats! I never saw the like. And looky there. I count nine of them. And they're carrying one little dead cat on a stretcher. Never saw that before!

2

Narrator:
The woodcutter was even more surprised when one of the cats spoke to him.

3

First Cat:
Say, mister. Would you please tell Aunt Kan that Polly Grundy is dead?

4

Woodcutter: *(Shaking his head and speaking to himself)*
If that don't take all! Whoever heard of cats talking? Who is this Aunt Kan? And who is this Polly Grundy? Sure beats all.

5

Second Cat:
Hey, mister. Please tell Aunt Kan that Polly Grundy is dead.

6

Narrator:
This was enough for the woodcutter. He broke into a run. He never stopped until he got home. That night he and his wife were sitting in front of the fire eating their supper. Their yellow cat dozed on the rug.

7

Wife:
Well, old man, you sure are quiet. Didn't anything happen today worth talking about?

8

Woodcutter:
Well, something did happen. But it surely was strange. I wasn't going to tell you. You'll think I've gone plumb crazy.

9

Wife:
Well, it's clear something's on your mind. You may as well tell it.

10

From *Scary Readers Theatre*. © 1994 Suzanne I. Barchers. Teacher Ideas Press. P.O. Box 6633, Englewood, CO 80155. 1-800-237-6124.

Woodcutter:
Well, when I was walking home I came upon nine black cats. They were carrying a dead little cat on a stretcher.   11

Wife:
What are you talking about? You must have been in the sun too long.   12

Woodcutter:
That wasn't the strangest part. These cats talked to me.   13

Wife:
Now I'm beginning to wonder if you *have* gone daft.   14

Woodcutter:
No, it's true. They kept asking me to tell Aunt Kan that Polly Grundy is dead.   15

Narrator:
With that, their yellow cat jumped up from the rug.   16

Yellow Cat:
Is Polly Grundy dead? By golly, then I must go to the burying!   17

Narrator:
Out the door that yellow cat flew. And it has never come back!   18

From *Scary Readers Theatre*. © 1994 Suzanne I. Barchers. Teacher Ideas Press. P.O. Box 6633, Englewood, CO 80155. 1-800-237-6124.

The Grave

SUMMARY

In this short piece of American folklore, a young girl stands on a grave and is frightened to death.
Reading level: 2.

PRESENTATION SUGGESTIONS

All characters can stand on stage in order of the reading.

PROPS

A mural of a graveyard could be in the background. A jackknife could be placed on a stool near the front of the stage.

CHARACTERS

Narrator
First Girl
First Boy
Second Girl
Second Boy

From *Scary Readers Theatre.* © 1994 Suzanne I. Barchers. Teacher Ideas Press. P.O. Box 6633, Englewood, CO 80155. 1-800-237-6124.

The Grave

Narrator:
    One night four teenagers were having a party. To get to the house where the party was to be held, they had to walk by a graveyard.   1

First Girl:
    I hate walking by that graveyard. It's creepy.   2

First Boy:
    Well, I don't mind walking by it, but I'd never walk *through* the graveyard at night.   3

Second Girl:
    Why? What could possibly happen to you? Everyone there is dead.   4

First Boy:
    Don't you know that if you stand on a grave the person inside will pull you in?   5

First Girl:
    That's just a silly superstition.   6

Second Girl:
    That's right. You're just trying to scare us.   7

Second Boy:
    No, it's true. In fact, I'll give ten dollars to anyone who is brave enough to stand on a grave at night.   8

Second Girl:
    I'll take that bet. I'm not afraid of any grave. And I could sure use the money. I'll go tonight!   9

First Boy:
    Well, I'm not going to go at night. How will we know if she has really stood on the grave?   10

Second Boy:
    Here, take my knife. Put it in the ground in the middle of the grave, and tomorrow I'll go get it. If you really stood on the grave, that will prove it.   11

From *Scary Readers Theatre*. © 1994 Suzanne I. Barchers. Teacher Ideas Press. P.O. Box 6633, Englewood, CO 80155. 1-800-237-6124.

Narrator:

The girl took the knife and left. She was nervous but kept telling herself that 12
nothing in the graveyard could hurt her. Finally, she got to the first grave. She
stood quietly on the grave for a moment.

Second Girl:

Well, this isn't so bad. I guess I'll put the knife in the ground now. 13

Narrator:

She bent over, plunged the knife into the soil, and began to leave, but she 14
couldn't get away. Something was holding her back!

Second Girl:

Something has got me! 15

Narrator:

She screamed, but no one heard her. She tried to get away, but something was 16
holding her fast. When she didn't come back to the party, the others got worried.

First Girl:

I think we should go look for her. It's gotten awfully late. She should have been 17
back by now.

First Boy:

Let me get a flashlight. We'll go look for her. 18

Narrator:

When they got to the grave, they shined the flashlight on the young girl's body. 19
The knife was stuck through her skirt, pinning her to the ground. She had died
of fright.

The Hobyahs

SUMMARY

In this English tale, a little dog saves a family from the hobyahs (hobby-ahs) until the old man kills the dog. The hobyahs eat the old man and old woman, and then they kidnap the little girl, who is rescued by a hunter.
Reading level: 2.

PRESENTATION SUGGESTIONS

The narrator should stand to one side. There should be at least three hobyahs reading in unison. The girl and old man can stay on stage throughout, and the old woman can be added for a nonspeaking part. The hunter can enter for his lines.

PROPS

The stage could have cornstalks in the corner and a stuffed toy dog.

CHARACTERS

Narrator

Hobyahs (three or more)

Old Man

Hunter

Girl

The Hobyahs

Narrator:
Once there were an old man, an old woman, and a little girl who all lived in a little house made of hempstalks. They also had a little dog. Some ugly hobyahs lived nearby, and one night they stomped around the little house.

1

Hobyahs:
Hobyahs! Hobyahs! Hobyahs!
Tear down the hempstalk house.
Eat the old man and old woman!
Carry off the little girl!

2

Narrator:
Now the little dog heard the ruckus and began to bark. The old man woke up.

3

Old Man:
That little dog barks so much that I can't get my sleep. Tomorrow I will cut off its tail!

4

Narrator:
The barking scared off the hobyahs, but the next morning the old man cut off the little dog's tail. That night the ugly hobyahs came again and stomped around the little house.

5

Hobyahs:
Hobyahs! Hobyahs! Hobyahs!
Tear down the hempstalk house.
Eat the old man and old woman!
Carry off the little girl!

6

Narrator:
Again the little dog heard the ruckus and began to bark. The old man woke up.

7

Old Man:
That little dog barks so much that I can't get my sleep. Tomorrow I will cut off one of its legs!

8

Narrator:
The barking scared off the hobyahs, but the next morning the old man cut off one of the little dog's legs. That night, the ugly hobyahs came again and stomped around the little house.

9

From *Scary Readers Theatre*. © 1994 Suzanne I. Barchers. Teacher Ideas Press. P.O. Box 6633, Englewood, CO 80155. 1-800-237-6124.

Hobyahs:

Hobyahs! Hobyahs! Hobyahs!   10
Tear down the hempstalk house.
Eat the old man and old woman!
Carry off the little girl!

Narrator:

Again the little dog heard the ruckus and began to bark. The old man woke up.   11

Old Man:

That little dog barks so much that I can't get my sleep. Tomorrow I will cut off   12
another one of its legs!

Narrator:

The barking scared off the hobyahs, but the next morning the old man cut off   13
another of the little dog's legs. That night the ugly hobyahs came again and
stomped around the little house.

Hobyahs:

Hobyahs! Hobyahs! Hobyahs!   14
Tear down the hempstalk house.
Eat the old man and old woman!
Carry off the little girl!

Narrator:

Again the little dog heard the ruckus and began to bark. The old man woke up.   15

Old Man:

That little dog barks so much that I can't get my sleep. Tomorrow I will cut off   16
another one of its legs!

Narrator:

The barking scared off the hobyahs, but the next morning the old man cut off   17
another one of the little dog's legs. That night the ugly hobyahs came again and
stomped around the little house.

Hobyahs:

Hobyahs! Hobyahs! Hobyahs!   18
Tear down the hempstalk house.
Eat the old man and old woman!
Carry off the little girl!

Narrator:

Again the little dog heard the ruckus and began to bark. The old man woke up.   19

Old Man:

That little dog barks so much that I can't get my sleep. Tomorrow I will cut off   20
the last of its legs!

Narrator:

The barking scared off the hobyahs, but the next morning the old man cut off   21
the last of the little dog's legs. That night the ugly hobyahs came again and
stomped around the little house.

Hobyahs:

Hobyahs! Hobyahs! Hobyahs!   22
Tear down the hempstalk house.
Eat the old man and old woman!
Carry off the little girl!

Narrator:

Again the little dog heard the ruckus and began to bark. The old man woke up.   23

Old Man:

That little dog barks so much that I can't get my sleep. Tomorrow I will cut off   24
its head!

Narrator:

The barking scared off the hobyahs, but the next morning the old man cut off   25
the little dog's head. That night the ugly hobyahs came again and stomped
around the little house.

Hobyahs:

Hobyahs! Hobyahs! Hobyahs!   26
Tear down the hempstalk house.
Eat the old man and old woman!
Carry off the little girl!

Narrator:

The little dog was dead, so nothing scared off the hobyahs. They tore down the   27
house. They ate the old man and old woman. They put the girl in a big burlap
bag and took her to their den. They opened the bag and looked in at the girl.

From *Scary Readers Theatre*. © 1994 Suzanne I. Barchers. Teacher Ideas Press. P.O. Box 6633, Englewood, CO 80155. 1-800-237-6124.

Hobyahs: *(Gleefully)*
   Look at us!   28

Narrator:
   The little girl cried. But the hobyahs, full from their meal, went to sleep. The   29
   little girl kept crying. A hunter with a big black dog came along and heard her
   crying. He came in their den, saw the sack, and looked inside.

Hunter:
   Why are you crying?   30

Girl:
   The hobyahs ate the old man and old woman. I think they will eat me too!   31

Hunter:
   Don't worry. I'll take care of this.   32

Narrator:
   The hunter put his dog in the bag and took the girl to his home. The next night   33
   the hobyahs opened the bag.

Hobyahs: *(Gleefully)*
   Look at us!   34

Narrator:
   The big dog jumped out and ate all the hobyahs. And that is why there are no   35
   hobyahs today.

From *Scary Readers Theatre.* © 1994 Suzanne I. Barchers. Teacher Ideas Press. P.O. Box 6633, Englewood, CO 80155. 1-800-237-6124.

The Strange Hotel

SUMMARY

In this American ghost story, many strange things happen when the Tucker family stays at a hotel. When they leave the next morning, they discover the hotel has disappeared.
Reading level: 2.

PRESENTATION SUGGESTIONS

The narrator can be to the side, with the Tucker children in front of their parents. The old man and maid could enter and exit for their parts.

PROPS

Consider adding suitcases, a camera, dance music, pillows, a desk bell, and other hotel items.

CHARACTERS

Narrator

Mrs. Tucker

Mr. Tucker

Tommy

Old Man

Tammy

Maid

From *Scary Readers Theatre.* © 1994 Suzanne I. Barchers. Teacher Ideas Press. P.O. Box 6633, Englewood, CO 80155. 1-800-237-6124.

The Strange Hotel

Narrator:
    The Tucker family was taking a trip. It had gotten late and foggy, and they were
tired. Finally, they saw a hotel in the mist. The sign said "vacancy."   1

Mrs. Tucker:
    Let's stop here. This looks good enough for me.   2

Mr. Tucker:
    I'll get the bags. Tammy and Tommy, you help your mother.   3

Narrator:
    As the Tuckers got out of the car, the front door of the hotel opened.   4

Tommy:
    That's strange. No one's there.   5

Narrator:
    The family went to the front desk. An old man sat there.   6

Old Man:
    Welcome to our hotel.   7

Mrs. Tucker:
    May we have a room?   8

Old Man:
    Of course. Bellhop, show them to room 13.   9

Narrator:
    No bellhop showed up, but their bags rose through the air. The Tuckers followed
their bags.   10

Tammy:
    Mother, I don't like this place.   11

Mr. Tucker:
    I think we're all just a bit tired. Let's just go to our room and get some sleep.   12

From *Scary Readers Theatre.* © 1994 Suzanne I. Barchers. Teacher Ideas Press. P.O. Box 6633, Englewood, CO 80155. 1-800-237-6124.

Narrator:
    The door opened, and the Tuckers' bags were carefully set inside.   13

Mrs. Tucker:
    This is very strange. I guess I should offer a tip.   14

Narrator:
    Mrs. Tucker's dollar bill quickly disappeared, and the door closed quietly. The   15
    Tuckers began to get ready for bed, but they heard some music.

Tammy:
    Listen to that music! Can we go find it?   16

Mr. Tucker:
    It's so late.   17

Tommy:
    Please, Mom and Dad? We'll only stay a little while.   18

Mrs. Tucker:
    Well, I suppose. But come back in fifteen minutes.   19

Narrator:
    Tommy and Tammy went down the hall, following the sound of the music.   20

Tommy:
    It sounds like it's coming from this room.   21

Tammy:
    Let's open the door.   22

Narrator:
    When they opened the door, they saw a big room full of people dancing. But   23
    they could see right through all the people!

Tommy:
    This is too strange.   24

Tammy:
    It's creepy. Let's go.   25

Tommy:
Wait, Tammy. Here's another door. Let's peek in there. 26

Narrator:
When they opened this door, they saw a room full of people eating delicious food. Once again, they could see right through all the people. 27

Tammy:
I've seen enough. Let's go back to our room. 28

Tommy:
You're right. 29

Narrator:
Tommy and Tammy went back to their room. 30

Mrs. Tucker:
What did you find? 31

Tammy:
Well, we found the dancers, but they didn't look right. 32

Tommy:
And then we found some people eating, but they didn't look right either. 33

Mr. Tucker:
Well, we are all pretty tired from the trip. Let's just go to sleep now. 34

Narrator:
The next morning, the Tuckers were awakened by a knock at the door. 35

Mrs. Tucker:
Who's there? 36

Maid:
It's the maid. I'm here with your breakfast. 37

Mr. Tucker:
Well, that's very nice. Come on in. 38

From *Scary Readers Theatre.* © 1994 Suzanne I. Barchers. Teacher Ideas Press. P.O. Box 6633, Englewood, CO 80155. 1-800-237-6124.

Maid:

I hope you find everything to your liking. I'll be back in an hour to take the 39
dishes and clean your room.

Mrs. Tucker:

Thank you kindly. 40

Mr. Tucker:

Dear, did you notice anything strange about her? 41

Mrs. Tucker:

Well, she hardly seemed to be there. But I didn't have my glasses on. 42

Narrator:

The Tuckers ate their breakfast and packed their bags. They went downstairs, 43
but no one was at the front desk. They rang the bell, but no one appeared.

Mrs. Tucker:

I guess I'll just leave this money in an envelope. 44

Mr. Tucker:

Tammy and Tommy, you get in the car. We'll be right along. 45

Narrator:

The Tuckers all got in the car, ready to continue their trip. They began to drive 46
down the road.

Mr. Tucker:

Wait, dear. We forgot to take a picture of our hotel. Go back so I can get a good 47
shot of it.

Narrator:

When Mr. Tucker turned the car around, they all gasped with shock. Instead of 48
a hotel, there was nothing but an empty lot. They got out and looked more
closely. On the ground lay their envelope of money.

From *Scary Readers Theatre.* © 1994 Suzanne I. Barchers. Teacher Ideas Press. P.O. Box 6633, Englewood, CO 80155. 1-800-237-6124.

The Wolf and the Seven Little Kids

SUMMARY

A nanny goat has seven kids in this tale by the Brothers Grimm. She warns her children about letting the wolf in the house, but the wolf tricks them. It eats all but the youngest kid who has hidden in the clock case. When the mother comes home and finds her kid, they search together for the wolf, cut open its belly, and find her other kids whole and alive. They fill the wolf's belly with stones, and it drowns.

Reading level: 2.

PRESENTATION SUGGESTIONS

This script offers an opportunity to involve many students. Choose seven students to represent the seven kids, with one of the seven designated as the youngest kid. The participants can read while standing. The seven kids can read as a group. The mother can enter for her readings.

PROPS

Consider placing the following items on the stage: chalk, cupboard, table, washtub, clock, pillows, blanket, and stones. The mother might wear a bell to distinguish her from the kids.

CHARACTERS

> Narrator
>
> Mother
>
> Six Kids
>
> Wolf
>
> Youngest Kid

The Wolf and the Seven Little Kids

Narrator:

There was once a nanny goat who had seven kids. She loved them dearly. One day she was going into the woods to fetch some food for them. She called them to her.   1

Mother:

Children, I am going into the woods for some food. Watch out for the wolf. If he gets in the house, he will eat you up. He may try to trick you. But you will know him by his gruff voice and black feet.   2

Seven Kids:

We'll be careful, Mother.   3

Narrator:

The nanny goat went off to the woods. Soon the kids heard knocking and a voice at the door.   4

Wolf:

Open the door, dear children. Your mother is back. I have something for each of you.   5

Narrator:

The kids knew that wasn't their mother's voice.   6

Seven Kids:

You are not our mother! She has a soft voice. You are the wolf!   7

Narrator:

The wolf went to a shop and bought a lump of chalk. He ate it, and his voice became very soft. Soon the kids heard knocking again and a voice at the door.   8

Wolf:

Open the door, dear children. Your mother is back. I have something for each of you.   9

Narrator:

But the wolf had unwittingly put his black paws on the windowsill.   10

From *Scary Readers Theatre*. © 1994 Suzanne I. Barchers. Teacher Ideas Press. P.O. Box 6633, Englewood, CO 80155. 1-800-237-6124.

Seven Kids:

    You are not our mother! She doesn't have black paws. You are the wolf!   11

Narrator:

    The wolf went to the baker.   12

Wolf:

    I have hurt my feet. Put some dough on them.   13

Narrator:

    After the baker had put some dough on his feet, the wolf went to the miller.   14

Wolf:

    Put some flour on my feet.   15

Narrator:

    The miller suspected that the wolf was up to no good. But when he hesitated,   16
the wolf said he would eat him up. So the miller put the flour on the wolf's feet.
The wolf hurried to the home of the nanny goat. Soon the kids heard knocking
and a voice at the door.

Wolf:

    Open the door, dear children. Your mother is back. I have something for each   17
of you.

Narrator:

    This time, when the kids heard the soft voice and saw the white feet on the   18
windowsill, they thought it was their mother. They opened the door. When the
wolf came in, they tried to hide. One ran under the table. The second jumped
into bed. The third hid in the oven. The fourth ran in the kitchen. The fifth went
into the cupboard. The sixth hid in the washtub. The seventh hid in the tall clock
case. But it was too late. The wolf swallowed each one except the seventh. He
could not find him in the clock case. The wolf left, lay down in a nearby
meadow, and began to snore.

      The nanny goat came home. The house was ruined. Tables and chairs were
upside down. The washtub was broken. The bedcovers were torn from the bed.
She called for each of her kids by name. When she called for her youngest, he
answered.

From *Scary Readers Theatre*. © 1994 Suzanne I. Barchers. Teacher Ideas Press. P.O. Box 6633, Englewood, CO 80155. 1-800-237-6124.

Youngest Kid:
 I am here in the clock case, Mother.   19

Mother:
 Oh, my child! What has happened here? Where are your brothers and sisters?   20

Youngest Kid:
 The wolf tricked us. He ate everyone except me. I was hiding in the clock case,   21
 and the wolf didn't find me.

Narrator:
 After weeping for her lost ones, the nanny goat decided that perhaps the wolf   22
 had not gone very far. She and the youngest kid went outside. Soon they heard
 the snoring from the meadow. They looked carefully at the sleeping wolf and
 saw movement inside its belly.

Mother:
 Do you think my kids are still alive in the wolf?   23

Youngest Kid:
 Something is moving inside him, Mother.   24

Narrator:
 So she cut a hole in the wolf's belly, and out jumped all six kids. The mother   25
 joyfully danced around with them.

Mother:
 Now, my children. Fetch me some big stones. We will fill the wolf's body so   26
 he won't eat anyone else.

Narrator:
 The kids brought the stones and filled the wolf's belly. Their mother sewed the   27
 wolf up very tight. When he woke, he felt very thirsty and went to the stream
 to drink. When he bent over to drink, the heavy stones pulled him into the
 stream. The wolf drowned.

Seven Kids and Mother:
 The wolf is dead! The wolf is dead!   28

Narrator:
 The mother and her kids lived happily from that day forward.   29

From *Scary Readers Theatre*. © 1994 Suzanne I. Barchers. Teacher Ideas Press. P.O. Box 6633, Englewood, CO 80155. 1-800-237-6124.

Part 2

Bolster

Bolster

SUMMARY

In this English tale, an evil giant named Bolster kills each of his wives after one year of marriage. However, his last wife appeals to St. Agnes for help and outwits Bolster.
Reading level: 3.

PRESENTATION SUGGESTIONS

The narrator should be to the side, with Bolster and the wife center stage. St. Agnes could enter for her lines.

PROPS

Props could include a knife and real or mock rocks. The wife might be dressed nicely, with Bolster in rough clothes. St. Agnes could wear a cross.

CHARACTERS

Narrator

Bolster

Wife

St. Agnes

Bolster

Narrator:
There once lived a giant named Bolster who could tolerate a wife for no more than one year at a time. At the end of that year, he would take his wife to the top of St. Agnes's hill and stone her to death with huge rocks.

Bolster was in the habit of cleansing himself before his yearly killing. He would go to an open mine shaft, open a vein in his arm, and bleed until the mine shaft filled with blood. Then he would close the wound and return home feeling refreshed and rested. Then he would kill his wife. This time Bolster had taken his thousandth wife, and their year together was drawing to a close.

1

Bolster:
You have been a good, hardworking wife, but your year is nearly gone.

2

Wife:
Bolster, surely I can make you happy for another year. Won't you let me try?

3

Bolster:
Ah, you have been fine, but I can't change my ways now.

4

Narrator:
The wife decided there had to be a way to save herself, so she went to the top of St. Agnes's hill and appealed to the saint herself.

5

Wife:
Please, St. Agnes, can you help me? I don't think I should have to give up my life just to satisfy this giant's yearly ritual.

6

St. Agnes:
I will tell you how to save yourself, but are you willing to kill the giant?

7

Wife:
If that is the only way, then yes, I am.

8

St. Agnes:
Then listen to me.

9

Narrator:
St. Agnes told her what to do. The very next day the wife was ready for Bolster.

10

Wife:

Dear husband, I know you must cleanse yourself before we go to St. Agnes's 11
hill. May I help you prepare?

Bolster:

That would be fine. Let's be on our way then. 12

Narrator:

They set out toward St. Agnes's hill, but Bolster's wife led him to a different 13
mine shaft.

Wife:

I noticed this mine shaft just the other day. There is such a pretty view of the 14
sea here. Does it meet your needs?

Bolster:

It doesn't matter which mine shaft I use. This is fine. 15

Narrator:

Bolster took out his knife, opened his vein, and let the blood flow. He lay back, 16
looking at the sea, thinking of how much he would enjoy stoning his wife to
death later. Meanwhile, she hummed softly and stroked his brow as he bled.
After some time, Bolster noticed that the sea was no longer blue but was
streaked with red. He looked into the mine shaft and saw that it was not filling
up as usual.

Bolster: *(Angrily)*

You! You have tricked me! I will kill you now! 17

Narrator:

The giant staggered to his feet, but he was so weakened by the loss of blood 18
that he fell down. Moments later he was dead. His wife went home and every
day thereafter gave thanks to St. Agnes for her help.

Brave Heart

SCARIEST!!!

SUMMARY

In this tale from South America, an evil witch regularly raids a village for animals to satisfy her tremendous appetite. When Brave Heart decides to teach her a lesson, he is captured by the witch who intends to enslave him after eating her old slave, a young girl. Together the girl and Brave Heart escape, outwitting and killing the witch.
Reading level: 3.

PRESENTATION SUGGESTIONS

Because the villagers only have brief roles, they can leave the stage after their parts. The other characters can remain centered on the stage.

PROPS

Possible props include a fishing net, plastic or wooden fish and turtles, a mural of a tree and pond, a red stone, and a pouch stuffed with sand or confetti.

CHARACTERS

Narrator

Brave Heart

First Villager

Second Villager

Witch

Girl

Brave Heart

Narrator:

Once upon a time an evil witch lived in a great, green forest. She was very old but   1
was a strong runner with a voracious appetite. She would go boldly into the village
and steal chickens, pigs, and cows to eat, and no one could stop her. Finally, the people
got so desperate they created a special pen, and each villager contributed animals that
the witch could help herself to whenever she got hungry. One year, it became time
for a young man to bring some of his animals to the pen, but he refused to do it.

Brave Heart:

I raised these animals, and I care for them. I refuse to give them to that evil   2
witch. She is like a vampire bat drinking our blood.

First Villager:

You'd best be careful what you say. She will hear about you and punish you.   3

Brave Heart:

I'm not afraid of that old hag. Let her come. In fact, I think I will go into the   4
forest and teach her a lesson.

Second Villager:

He may be a bit foolish, but that young man has a brave heart.   5

Narrator:

And that is what they called him, Brave Heart, as they watched him head into   6
the forest. Brave Heart walked for two days, finally falling asleep under a tree
near a large pond. During the night, he had so many scary dreams that he
climbed up onto a branch of the tree to sleep. The next morning he woke to the
sound of someone singing in a cracking voice.

Witch:

Things in the water,   7
You belong to me.
Your lives are now over,
You're no longer free.

Things in the water,
Come here to me.
I'll kill you and eat you.
As quick as can be!

From *Scary Readers Theatre*. © 1994 Suzanne I. Barchers. Teacher Ideas Press. P.O. Box 6633, Englewood, CO 80155. 1-800-237-6124.

Narrator:

Brave Heart saw that it was the evil witch, singing a magical spell that made
the water animals swim straight into her net. Feeling tired and weak, Brave
Heart decided to stay hidden in the tree until he had a plan, but the witch looked
up, spied him, and smiled.

8

Witch:

You look hungry, my friend. Why don't you join me for breakfast? I have plenty
to eat.

9

Brave Heart:

Thank you, ma'am, but I'm fine right here.

10

Narrator:

When the witch saw he wouldn't come down, she began to pluck grass, placing
it in a pile. She sprinkled a magic powder on it and chanted her spell.

11

Witch:

To the tree, now,
Creep and crawl.
Up the trunk go,
One and all.

12

To the branch
Where the man does cling.
And to him
Pain and torture bring!

Pinch him, bite him,
One and all,
Until he must
In the water fall!

Narrator:

Each blade of grass changed into a large brown ant and crawled straight up the
trunk of Brave Heart's tree. When they swarmed all over him, pinching and
biting, Brave Heart let go of the branch and fell into the pond.

13

Witch:

Things in the water,
Come here to me.

14

Narrator:

Brave Heart was tangled in the net with fish, frogs, and other pond creatures, 15
and the witch dragged them all onto the bank. Then the witch stuffed them all
into a large bag, dragged it home, and threw Brave Heart into a tiny room. Later
the door opened, and Brave Heart saw a young girl in the doorway.

Brave Heart:

Who are you? 16

Girl:

I am the witch's slave, but you are to be her next slave. Now I will be killed 17
and eaten. That is her way.

Brave Heart:

This can't be happening. I can't let her eat you! We must escape. But what am 18
I saying? I couldn't even get away from her in the woods. She is just too strong
and fast.

Girl:

There may be a way. She has a magic stone that she uses for flying. She rarely 19
uses it because she can run nearly as fast, and it only works in the sunlight. I
know where she hides it, but I've never taken it because I knew that I couldn't
get away alone. Maybe if we work together we can escape. She's off gathering
firewood, so I can get the stone if you are willing to try. Maybe we can get
enough of a head start that she won't be able to catch us.

Brave Heart:

Yes! Get the stone, and let's at least try to escape! 20

Narrator:

The girl quickly returned with the stone and a bag of yellow powder. 21

Girl:

The witch uses this powder to change things from one kind to another. Maybe 22
it will help us.

Narrator:

Just then they were startled to hear the witch approaching. 23

From *Scary Readers Theatre*. © 1994 Suzanne I. Barchers. Teacher Ideas Press. P.O. Box 6633, Englewood, CO 80155. 1-800-237-6124.

Witch:

    I have the firewood, my dear. It is just dry enough to make a perfect fire to roast   24
you. Then I will teach the boy how to be my slave.

Brave Heart:

    Quick, we must hurry before she comes into the house.   25

Narrator:

    Brave Heart and the girl held hands while the girl said the magic words to make   26
the stone fly. They flew right out the window, past the witch who was about to
come in the front door. The witch began to run after them, staying just below
them. They flew on and on, but the witch kept up with them. Soon the sun would
set, and the stone would lose its power.

Brave Heart:

    We must do something quickly, or she will catch us.   27

Girl:

    Drop some of the powder and see what happens.   28

Narrator:

    When the powder fell on a bush, the leaves changed into rabbits. Always   29
hungry, the witch decided she could spare the time to eat just a few, so Brave
Heart and the girl gained a bit of distance on the witch. But as the sun began to
set, the power of the stone started to fail, and they flew lower and lower.

Girl:

    Soon we will be so low the witch will be able to catch us. What shall we do?   30

Brave Heart:

    I see the pond ahead. If we just hang on long enough, maybe she won't be able   31
to swim across the pond.

Girl:

    But she can swim just as fast as she can run!   32

Brave Heart:

    Let's try the powder again.   33

Narrator:

This time the powder changed some rocks at the edge of the pond into big   34
turtles. Once again, the greedy witch stopped to eat, swallowing many big
turtles, shells and all. Just as Brave Heart and the girl crossed the pond, the
magic stone gave out, and they drifted down to the ground. They watched as
the witch began to swim to them.

Witch:

You thought you could get away, but now I have you!   35

Girl:

Now she will kill me for sure.   36

Brave Heart:

Maybe not. Look, she is slowing down.   37

Girl:

It's the turtles she ate! They are too heavy for her!   38

Brave Heart:

You're right! She is drowning!   39

Narrator:

As they watched, the witch howled with fury and slowly sank to the bottom of   40
the pond. Brave Heart and the girl went back to the village where no one ever
worried again about the evil witch.

From *Scary Readers Theatre*. © 1994 Suzanne I. Barchers. Teacher Ideas Press. P.O. Box 6633, Englewood, CO 80155. 1-800-237-6124.

The Girl with the Lavender Dress

SUMMARY

In this favorite American ghost story, two young men come upon a young girl walking along the road. They take her with them to a dance and then to her home. When they return the next day for a forgotten jacket, they discover she was a ghost.
Reading level: 3.

PRESENTATION SUGGESTIONS

Because there are only five characters, all five can remain on stage, with the narrator to the side, the young men and Lavender in the center, and the old woman to the other side.

PROPS

Props might include a lavender dress, a mural of a graveyard, and a jacket.

CHARACTERS

Narrator
First Young Man
Second Young Man
Lavender
Old Woman

The Girl with the Lavender Dress

Narrator:
Two young men were going to a dance on a Saturday night. They drove along a country road where they unexpectedly saw a lovely young girl in a lavender dress walking alone.

1

First Young Man:
I wonder what she is doing out here all alone?

2

Second Young Man:
Let's stop and see if she'll ride with us.

3

First Young Man:
Good evening, miss. We were wondering if you would like a ride.

4

Lavender:
Thank you. I would, if you don't mind.

5

Narrator:
Soon they were all talking like old friends and having a great time.

6

First Young Man:
You sure are a lot of fun. What is your name anyway?

7

Lavender:
Everyone calls me by my nickname, Lavender.

8

Second Young Man:
How did you get that nickname?

9

Lavender:
Probably because it's my favorite color.

10

First Young Man:
Well, Lavender, how about coming along to the dance with us?

11

Second Young Man:
Come on, Lavender. It'll be lots of fun.

12

From *Scary Readers Theatre*. © 1994 Suzanne I. Barchers. Teacher Ideas Press. P.O. Box 6633, Englewood, CO 80155. 1-800-237-6124.

Lavender:

All right, but you'll need to drive me home afterward.

13

Narrator:

The two young men had a wonderful time taking turns dancing with Lavender. She was the prettiest girl there, dancing nonstop all evening long. Soon the dance was over, and it was time to go home.

14

First Young Man:

Well, time to get you home, Lavender. It's a bit chilly outside now. Why don't you put on my jacket?

15

Lavender:

Thank you. You're very kind.

16

Narrator:

Lavender gave the young men directions to a run-down little house, and when they arrived, she slipped quickly out of the car and ran inside. The men realized she still wore the borrowed jacket, but because the house was dark they decided to return for it the next day. When they returned, they found the house and knocked loudly on the door. Finally, an old woman came to the door.

17

First Young Man:

Good afternoon, ma'am. We were wondering if we could see Lavender for a minute.

18

Old Woman:

What are you talking about? Is this your idea of a joke?

19

Second Young Man:

Of course not. My friend just wants to get his jacket back.

20

Old Woman:

You boys must have great imaginations. Lavender's been dead for ten years.

21

First Young Man:

That can't be. There must be some mix-up. The girl we're talking about went with us to a dance last night.

22

From *Scary Readers Theatre.* © 1994 Suzanne I. Barchers. Teacher Ideas Press. P.O. Box 6633, Englewood, CO 80155. 1-800-237-6124.

Old Woman:

Well, there is only one Lavender that I have ever known. She was my daughter   23
and she is buried at the church graveyard over yonder. She was walking along
that road on her way to a dance when she was hit by a car. Go see for yourselves.

Narrator:

The boys left and drove down the road toward the church.   24

Second Young Man:

There's the graveyard. Let's go take a look.   25

Narrator:

They looked around a bit and soon spotted a gravestone with the name Lavender   26
engraved on it.

On top of it, neatly folded, the men found the jacket.

From *Scary Readers Theatre*. © 1994 Suzanne I. Barchers. Teacher Ideas Press. P.O. Box 6633, Englewood, CO 80155. 1-800-237-6124.

Jack and His Master

SUMMARY

Jack's two older brothers are cheated and crippled by an evil master, the Gray Churl. Jack avenges them by repeatedly outwitting the master. Finally, when Jack has earned the right to mutilate the Gray Churl, the master pays Jack for all he and his brothers have earned.

Reading level: 3.

PRESENTATION SUGGESTIONS

Because Jack, the narrator, and the Gray Churl have long parts, they should be center stage, with the mother and the other sons exiting or sitting after their parts. The Gray Churl's wife could enter for her reading and then exit or sit.

PROPS

The country theme could be recreated with hay, a plow, a cowbell, corn stalks, or other appropriate items.

CHARACTERS

Narrator

Mother

Oldest Son

Middle Son

Jack

Gray Churl

Wife

Jack and His Master

Narrator:

A poor woman had three sons. The oldest and middle sons were clever fellows, but the youngest was called Jack the Fool because he was thought to be simple.

One day, the oldest son went away to work for a year. When he returned, he dragged one foot, his back was scarred, and his face was lined and weary.

1

Mother:

Son, what happened to you?

2

Oldest Son:

I went into service with the Gray Churl of the town of Mischance. The agreement was to work for twenty pounds and that whoever would first say he was sorry for the bargain would get an inch wide of skin, from shoulder to hips, taken off his back. If it was my master who was sorry, he would pay double wages. If it was me, I'd get no wages at all. He gave me little to eat and worked me so hard that I couldn't stand it. One day when he asked if I was sorry for my bargain, I was so mad I said yes. That is why I am disabled for life.

3

Middle Son:

We can't let this man go unpunished. I'll go take service with the Gray Churl and annoy him until he is sorry for the bargain. Then I'll love watching the skin come off his back!

4

Mother:

No, son, don't go. One loss is enough. This Gray Churl sounds evil.

5

Narrator:

But the middle son was determined to go. He went to see the Gray Churl and agreed to work with him for a year. The terms were the same as for his older brother, and in a year he was back and just as miserable as his brother.

6

Jack:

Mother, you can't stop me. I must go to this cruel man and avenge myself on him for my brothers.

7

Mother:

No, Jack. You are the only able-bodied man left in our family. Please stay. I need you here.

8

Narrator:

But Jack insisted on going, and soon he was striking the same bargain with the Gray Churl. 9

Gray Churl:

Now then, Jack, if you refuse to do anything you are able to do, you must lose a month's wages. 10

Jack:

That is satisfactory. But if you stop me from doing a thing after telling me to do it, you are to give me an additional month's wages. 11

Gray Churl:

I am satisfied. 12

Narrator:

The first day, Jack worked hard and was fed poorly. The next day, Jack came into the parlor just as the Gray Churl and his wife were taking the goose off the spit. Jack took out his knife, cut off a leg and thigh, and began to eat. 13

Gray Churl:

How dare you help yourself to that goose! 14

Jack:

But you agreed to feed me, and once I've eaten this goose, you won't need to feed me until tomorrow. Are you sorry for our agreement? 15

Gray Churl:

You're right. I'm not sorry. 16

Jack:

That's fine then. 17

Narrator:

The next day, Jack was to work on the bog, but the breakfast was not very big. He spoke to Gray Churl's wife. 18

Jack:

Ma'am, I think it would be best if I take my lunch with me so I won't lose time coming back from the bog. 19

Wife:
> That's true, Jack. Here's some cake, butter, and milk.   20

Narrator:
> But Jack stayed in his seat and ate everything she'd just given him.   21

Jack:
> Ma'am, I'll be able to go to work earlier tomorrow if I sleep out by the bog.   22
> You may as well give me my supper now.

Wife:
> Well, I guess you're right.   23

Narrator:
> The wife gathered together his supper, and he ate every bite on the spot. Then   24
> Jack went out to the stable and talked with the Gray Churl.

Jack:
> What do servants do here after they have eaten their supper?   25

Gray Churl:
> Nothing at all. They just go to sleep.   26

Narrator:
> So Jack went to the loft and lay down as if to sleep.   27

Gray Churl:
> You scoundrel, Jack. What do you mean by this?   28

Jack:
> Just to go to sleep. You see, your good wife gave me breakfast, lunch, and   29
> supper. And you yourself told me that bed followed supper. Do you blame me,
> sir?

Gray Churl:
> Yes I do, you rascal.   30

Jack:
> Then give me one pound thirteen and fourpence, please.   31

From *Scary Readers Theatre.* © 1994 Suzanne I. Barchers. Teacher Ideas Press. P.O. Box 6633, Englewood, CO 80155. 1-800-237-6124.

Gray Churl:
 And what for?   32

Jack:
 I see you've forgotten our bargain. Are you sorry for it?   33

Gray Churl:
 Oh . . . well . . . no. I'll give you the money after your nap. 34

Narrator:
 Early the next morning, Jack asked about his work for the day. 35

Gray Churl:
 Today you'll be holding the plow in that field.   36

Narrator:
 Later, the Gray Churl went to see how well Jack could plow, but all he saw was 37
 a little boy driving while Jack rode behind, holding onto the plow.

Gray Churl:
 What are you doing, Jack?   38

Jack:
 I'm holding this plow as you told me.   39

Gray Churl:
 You're not supposed to just hold the plow. You're supposed to plow the ground. 40

Jack:
 Well, I do wish you'd have told me. Do you blame me for what I have done? 41

Gray Churl:
 Just go and plow the ground, Jack.   42

Jack:
 Are you sorry for our agreement?   43

Gray Churl:
 Of course not.   44

From *Scary Readers Theatre.* © 1994 Suzanne I. Barchers. Teacher Ideas Press. P.O. Box 6633, Englewood, CO 80155. 1-800-237-6124.

Narrator:
So Jack plowed away for the rest of the day. The next day, the Gray Churl asked Jack to mind the cows in a field that was half full of young corn and half full of wheat.

45

Gray Churl:
Be sure to keep Browney from the wheat. If she's not in mischief, you won't need to worry about the others.

46

Narrator:
At noon, the Gray Churl went to check on Jack and found him asleep and Browney tied to a thorn tree. The other cows were tramping around and eating the wheat.

47

Gray Churl:
Jack, you fool. Don't you see what the cows are doing?

48

Jack:
Do you blame me, Master?

49

Gray Churl:
To be sure, you lazy lout, I do!

50

Jack:
Then pay me one pound thirteen and fourpence, Master. You said if I only kept Browney out of mischief the rest would stay out of harm. There she is, safely tied up. Are you sorry for hiring me, Master?

51

Gray Churl:
Of course not. I'll give you your money at dinner. Now, don't let a cow go out of the field or into the wheat the rest of the day.

52

Jack:
Never fear, Master.

53

Narrator:
The next day, the Gray Churl discovered that three heifers were missing.

54

Gray Churl:
Jack, go and search for those missing heifers.

55

From *Scary Readers Theatre*. © 1994 Suzanne I. Barchers. Teacher Ideas Press. P.O. Box 6633, Englewood, CO 80155. 1-800-237-6124.

Jack:

    And where would I search?   56

Gray Churl:

    Search every likely and unlikely place for them.   57

Narrator:

    The Gray Churl was amazed when he came in for dinner and found Jack pulling   58
thatch off the roof and peeking into the holes he was making.

Gray Churl:

    Just what are you doing?   59

Jack:

    Looking for the heifers.   60

Gray Churl:

    Why would they be there?   61

Jack:

    Well, you told me to look in the likely places, so I looked in the cowhouses,   62
pastures, and fields. Now I'm looking in the most unlikely places I can think
of. Maybe that isn't pleasing to you.

Gray Churl:

    Of course it isn't pleasing to me, you scoundrel.   63

Jack:

    Well, sir, then hand me one pound thirteen and fourpence before you sit down   64
to your dinner. I'm afraid you are sorry you hired me.

Gray Churl:

    No, no. I'm not sorry. Would you put the thatch back again, just as if you were   65
fixing your mother's cabin?

Jack:

    Of course, Master.   66

Narrator:

    And soon the roof was even better than before.   67

From *Scary Readers Theatre.* © 1994 Suzanne I. Barchers. Teacher Ideas Press. P.O. Box 6633, Englewood, CO 80155. 1-800-237-6124.

Gray Churl:
    Jack, go look for the heifers and bring them home.   68

Jack:
    Where should I look?   69

Gray Churl:
    Look for them as if they were your own.   70

Narrator:
    So Jack found the heifers and had them in the paddock by sunset. The next   71
    morning, the Gray Churl gave Jack his work for the day.

Gray Churl:
    Jack, the path across the bog to the pasture is very bad. The sheep sink in with   72
    every step. Go and make the sheep's feet a good path.

Narrator:
    Later, the Gray Churl went to check up on Jack and found him sharpening a   73
    carving knife while the sheep grazed around him.

Gray Churl:
    Jack, is this how you fix a path?   74

Jack:
    Everything needs a start. As my dear mother always says, something well begun   75
    is half done. I am sharpening the knife. Then I'll have the feet off every sheep
    in the flock.

Gray Churl:
    Are you daft, man? Why would you do that?   76

Jack:
    You yourself said to make a path with the feet of the sheep.   77

Gray Churl:
    You fool, I meant make a good path for the sheep's feet.   78

Jack:
    It's a pity you didn't say so. Hand me out one pound thirteen and fourpence if   79
    you don't want me to finish my job. Maybe you're sorry for your bargain?

From *Scary Readers Theatre*. © 1994 Suzanne I. Barchers. Teacher Ideas Press. P.O. Box 6633, Englewood, CO 80155. 1-800-237-6124.

Gray Churl:

To be sure I am! Well . . . not yet, that is.   80

Narrator:

The next night, the Gray Churl was going to a wedding.   81

Gray Churl:

Jack, I want to leave the party at midnight, so come and bring me home then.   82
If you get there before midnight, throw the sheep's eye at me, and I'll have them
give you some supper.

Narrator:

Now, throwing the sheep's eye used to mean to glance kindly, perhaps even   83
lovingly, at someone. But at about eleven o'clock, when the Gray Churl was in
great spirits, something clammy hit him on the cheek. It fell on the table, and
he saw it was the eye of a sheep. A minute later another one hit him. He hated
to be rude to the host, so he said nothing, but in two minutes, just as he was
about to take a bite of his dinner, another hit him right in the mouth.

Gray Churl:

My good host, who would do such a nasty thing as to throw this sheep's eye at me.   84

Jack:

Master, it was myself throwing those sheep's eyes, just as you asked. I just wanted 85
to drink to the bride and groom's health and came early, just as you bade me.

Gray Churl:

You are indeed a scamp. Where did you get these eyes?   86

Jack:

Why, from the heads of your own sheep, Master. I would never go to a   87
neighbor's and do such an evil thing to their sheep.

Gray Churl:

I rue the day I ever had the bad luck to meet you!   88

Jack: *(Loudly)*

You're all witness that my master says he is sorry he ever met me. My time here   89
is up. Master, hand me double wages and come into the next room and take off
your shirt. I am going to take a strip of skin off your back an inch wide from
your shoulder to your hip.

From *Scary Readers Theatre*. © 1994 Suzanne I. Barchers. Teacher Ideas Press. P.O. Box 6633, Englewood, CO 80155. 1-800-237-6124.

Narrator:

The people spoke out against such evil doings, but Jack shouted for quiet.　　90

Jack:

Wait! None of you stopped him when he took the same strips from the backs　　91
of my two brothers and sent them home penniless to their poor mother. Listen
to my side.

Narrator:

When Jack told the whole story, the people were ready to see justice done. The　　92
Gray Churl screamed for mercy, but the men held him down, removed his shirt,
and laid him on the floor in the next room. Jack had the carving knife in his
hand ready to begin and scraped the floor a few times.

Jack:

Now, you wicked villain. I'll make you an offer. Give me my double wages and　　93
two hundred guineas for my brothers, and I'll forget this business.

Gray Churl:

No! I'd let you skin me from head to foot before I'd give you all that money!　　94

Jack:

Here goes then.　　95

Narrator:

Jack grinned and cut just a small piece of skin.　　96

Gray Churl:

No! Wait! Stop your hand! I'll give you the money!　　97

Jack:

Now, my friends, you have all heard him. Don't think that I am such a bad sort. I　　98
got those sheep eyes from the butcher. I wouldn't have the heart to do this to a rat.

Narrator:

They all went into the other room and drank to Jack's health. Six stout fellows　　99
took Jack and the Gray Churl of Mischance home and waited until he had paid
Jack his wages.

　　When Jack got home, he was no longer Jack the Fool, but was called Skin
Churl Jack.

From *Scary Readers Theatre*. © 1994 Suzanne I. Barchers. Teacher Ideas Press. P.O. Box 6633, Englewood, CO 80155. 1-800-237-6124.

Raggelugg

SUMMARY

A little bunny learns to mind his mother after nearly being eaten by a snake.

Reading level: 3.

PRESENTATION SUGGESTIONS

The narrator should be to the side, with Raggelugg and Molly Cottontail in the center. The snake can enter and exit for its part.

PROPS

Young children might want to wear bunny ears, the snake could have a rattle, or students could put a mural of a meadow in the background.

CHARACTERS

> Narrator
>
> Molly Cottontail
>
> Raggelugg
>
> Snake

Raggelugg

Narrator:

Once upon a time, there was a little bunny rabbit named Raggelugg. He lived with his mother, Molly Cottontail. Their nest was in the middle of the meadow. Every morning, Raggelugg's mother would leave for a while to find food and water.

1

Molly Cottontail:

Raggelugg, I'm off to get something to eat and drink. You sit right here. Don't move a bit! I'll be back as quickly as I can.

2

Raggelugg:

All right, Mother.

3

Narrator:

So Raggelugg sat as quietly as a mouse until his mother came back. Every day, the same thing happened.

4

Molly Cottontail:

Raggelugg, I'm off to get something to eat and drink. You sit right here. Don't move a bit! I'll be back as quickly as I can.

5

Raggelugg:

All right, Momma.

6

Narrator:

But one day, Raggelugg was just enough bigger that if he stretched one ear, he could hear just a little bit. And if he raised one eyebrow, he could see the sky. Suddenly, he heard a noise, but it didn't sound like his mother returning.

7

Snake: *(Whispering)*

Rustle, rustle, rustle.

8

Raggelugg:

I wonder what that is. Maybe the breeze. I'll put up my other ear and listen.

9

Snake: *(Whispering)*

Swish, swish, swish.

10

From *Scary Readers Theatre.* © 1994 Suzanne I. Barchers. Teacher Ideas Press. P.O. Box 6633, Englewood, CO 80155. 1-800-237-6124.

Raggelugg:
That's odd. It sounds like someone moving in the grass, but there aren't any footsteps.

11

Snake:
Rattle, rattle, rattle.

12

Raggelugg:
Now what is that! I think I will have to get up on my hind feet and look. After all, I am a lot bigger now.

13

Narrator:
So Raggelugg sat up, and there was a big, black snake looking right at him!

14

Snake:
Hisssss! Hisssss!

15

Narrator:
The snake darted forward and caught Raggelugg by one long ear.

16

Raggelugg:
Momma! Momma! Help me!

17

Narrator:
Slowly, the snake wrapped itself around Raggelugg and began to squeeze.

18

Raggelugg: *(Getting softer)*
Momma! Momma! Help me!

19

Narrator:
Even though Raggelugg could hardly squeak, Molly Cottontail heard him. She hopped as fast as she could to her son. Though the snake hissed at her, she jumped into the air and kicked it with her hind foot. The snake let go of Raggelugg, but it grabbed Molly Cottontail!

20

Molly Cottontail:
Run, Raggelugg, run!

21

From *Scary Readers Theatre*. © 1994 Suzanne I. Barchers. Teacher Ideas Press. P.O. Box 6633, Englewood, CO 80155. 1-800-237-6124.

Narrator:

    And while Raggelugg ran, his mother pulled loose from the snake. She ran past 22
Raggelugg, and he followed her across the meadow, lickety-split. They made
a new nest under a gooseberry bush. The next morning, Molly Cottontail needed
to leave for a bit.

Molly Cottontail:

    Raggelugg, I'm off to get something to eat and drink. You sit right here. Don't 23
move a bit! I'll be back as quickly as I can.

Narrator:

    And this time, Raggelugg sat right there and never moved! 24

From *Scary Readers Theatre.* © 1994 Suzanne I. Barchers. Teacher Ideas Press. P.O. Box 6633, Englewood, CO 80155. 1-800-237-6124.

The Thieving Lad

SCARIER!!

SUMMARY

In this adaptation of an Irish tale, a young lad, deciding to pursue a life of robbery, apprentices himself to a master thief. His mother predicts he will end up hanging from the bridge of Dublin for his crimes. Although he is never caught, her words are prophetic.

Reading level: 3.

PRESENTATION SUGGESTIONS

This cautionary tale has an ironic twist that will horrify and amuse the audience. The narrator should be to the front at one side. The lad and master thief can remain centered in front. The mother, farmer, king, and wise man can exit after their readings, and the king's daughter can come on stage for her part.

PROPS

A hangman's rope would add foreboding to the story. Because part of the story takes place on Halloween, apples, nuts, and pumpkins could be arranged on stage.

CHARACTERS

Narrator

Mother

Lad

Master Thief

Farmer

King

Wise Man

Princess

The Thieving Lad

Narrator:

Once there was a young lad who lived with his mother. He was a clever boy, and she had saved her money to send him to school, but he didn't want to go to school.

1

Mother:

Son, it is time for you to think about school or a trade.

2

Lad:

Not for me, Mother. I don't want to work that hard. I intend to be a thief.

3

Mother:

Son, haven't you seen the thieves that end up hanging from the bridge of Dublin? Forget this idea and come to church.

4

Lad:

Ha! Sermons are not for me, but I promise you this. I will take on the first trade you hear when you leave the church.

5

Narrator:

The mother was comforted a bit by these words, and she left for church. When it was time for church to end, the lad hid himself in the path by the church. As his mother passed by, he changed his voice and called out to her.

6

Lad:

Robbery! Robbery! Robbery!

7

Narrator:

The lad ran home, where his mother found him relaxing by the fire.

8

Lad:

Well, what news have you? Has anyone mentioned a trade?

9

Mother: *(Slowly)*

Well, as I walked down the path, someone cried out "Robbery! Robbery! Robbery!" But that was all.

10

Lad:

Then that is to be my trade!

11

From *Scary Readers Theatre.* © 1994 Suzanne I. Barchers. Teacher Ideas Press. P.O. Box 6633, Englewood, CO 80155. 1-800-237-6124.

Mother:
   If so, your end will be by hanging from the bridge of Dublin.   12

Narrator:
   That night the mother hardly slept, worrying over the fate of her son. By   13
   morning, she had resigned herself to helping him and went to see the master
   thief.

Mother:
   Sir, my son is clever and wants to learn your trade. Will you be kind enough to   14
   teach him?

Master Thief:
   If he is clever, I am the teacher for him. Send him to me tonight after dark.   15

Mother:
   Tonight it is then. I will send him to you.   16

Narrator:
   The lad was overjoyed at the prospect of learning from the master. Every night,   17
   he went to his home and learned more wicked tricks. Soon, the lad went with
   him to watch, and finally the master thought he was ready to help with a robbery.

Master Thief:
   There is a rich farmer who has received a great deal of money for his fat cattle   18
   and is going to spend a little on some lean cattle. Tonight is Halloween, and
   everyone will be burning nuts and bobbing for apples. While everyone is out,
   we will hide in his loft and rob his chest.

Narrator:
   That night, they sneaked to the loft, and the master thief dozed off while the   19
   lad waited impatiently for the darkest part of the night. Becoming most impa-
   tient, the boy went out to the farmyard and turned loose the cows. While the
   people gathered them back to the farmyard, he went to the farmhouse and took
   a handful of nuts. He returned to the loft, and while the master thief slept he
   sewed the hem of the thief's coat to a heavy hide of a bull hanging nearby. Then
   he woke the thief.

Lad: *(Stretching)*
   I think I will crack a nut.   20

From *Scary Readers Theatre*. © 1994 Suzanne I. Barchers. Teacher Ideas Press. P.O. Box 6633, Englewood, CO 80155. 1-800-237-6124.

Master Thief:
No, no. They will hear you! 21

Lad:
I don't care. It's Halloween, and I want to crack some nuts. 22

Farmer: *(Loudly)*
Someone is cracking nuts in the loft. 23

Narrator:
The farmer ran up to the loft where the master thief was trying to run away. The 24
hide of the bull slowed him down.

Farmer: *(Loudly)*
Look! He is stealing my hide! 25

Narrator:
The farmer and all his friends ran after the thief, who managed to tear the hide 26
off and run to his hiding place. Meanwhile, the lad searched the house until he
found the chest, threw the money bags over his shoulders, and set out for the
master thief's house.

Master Thief: *(Angrily)*
Here you are, you scoundrel! I shall make you pay for this. 27

Lad: *(Calmly)*
You needn't worry. While they were chasing you, I found the gold. Here it is. 28

Master Thief:
Ahh, you are the better thief for sure. You have surely earned your half. 29

Narrator:
And so it went. They made quite a pair, each one trying to impress the other 30
with his cleverness. The lad loved the danger and excitement, eagerly recruiting
others to steal alongside him. Soon they had a band of thieves so fearsome that
the king called his wise man to him.

King:
Wise man, what shall we do? These thieves are terrorizing the land. 31

From *Scary Readers Theatre.* © 1994 Suzanne I. Barchers. Teacher Ideas Press. P.O. Box 6633, Englewood, CO 80155. 1-800-237-6124.

Wise Man:

It will take a plan as clever as their leader. Let's invite everyone in the countryside to a ball. Let it be known that your daughter will wear her finest jewels. Surely the leader won't resist a chance to dance with her and try to steal hers and the others' jewels. I am sure his poor manners will give him away.

32

King:

Ah, a fine plan. We will be able to capture him for sure.

33

Narrator:

The night of the ball came, and the thief and his followers joined the dance. But the lad was so charming and clever that the wise man could not discern him from the other guests. Indeed, the lad fell instantly in love with the king's daughter. She pleaded with her father to marry him, and unable to resist her pleas, the king finally agreed. Soon, the lad and the princess were married. A few days after the wedding, they were walking along a path that led to a bridge.

34

Lad:

Dear wife, what bridge is this?

35

Princess:

Why, this is the bridge of Dublin.

36

Lad:

Indeed? Whenever I played a trick on my mother, she would tell me I would end up hanging from the bridge of Dublin.

37

Princess:

Well, dear husband, if you want to fulfill her prophecy, I shall let you hang here. Just let me tie my handkerchief around your ankle, and I will hang you over the side.

38

Lad:

Ah, you are not strong enough for that!

39

Princess:

Oh, yes, I am. Here, just try.

40

Narrator:

She pleaded so prettily that he gave in and let her bind the handkerchief around his ankle. She hung him over the side, and they both laughed at her strength.   41

Lad:

Now pull me up, dear!   42

Princess:

All right, my husband.   43

Narrator:

But just as she began to pull him up, a great cry arose that the palace was burning. The princess turned around with a start and let go of the handkerchief. The lad fell, struck his head on a stone, and died instantly. And so his mother's prophecy came true after all.   44

From *Scary Readers Theatre*. © 1994 Suzanne I. Barchers. Teacher Ideas Press. P.O. Box 6633, Englewood, CO 80155. 1-800-237-6124.

The Three Dwarfs

SUMMARY

In this story by the Brothers Grimm, a young girl befriends three dwarfs who reward her. When the stepsister fails to be similarly rewarded, she and the stepmother try to revenge themselves on the girl, who is rescued by a king who marries her. Once again the stepmother and stepsister try to kill the girl, but are tricked into pronouncing their own sentence for their wickedness.

Reading level: 3.

PRESENTATION SUGGESTIONS

The characters could be ranged across the stage with the narrator, old woman, daughter, man, and stepsister to the front. The dwarfs could exit after their lines. The king, duck, and kitchen boy could enter for their lines. Because the duck is actually the daughter, one person could read both roles.

PROPS

Possible props could include a boot, gold pieces, pitchers, a basket, a broom, yarn, an ax, a plastic duck, or other items from the story.

CHARACTERS

Narrator

Stepmother

Daughter

Father

First Dwarf

Second Dwarf

Third Dwarf

Stepsister

King

Duck

Kitchen Boy

The Three Dwarfs

Narrator:

Once there were a widow and widower who each had a daughter. The daughters were friends and often walked together. One day, the widow spoke to the man's daughter.

1

Stepmother:

Listen to me. Tell your father I would like to marry him. If we marry, you will wash in milk every morning and drink wine. My daughter will wash in water and drink water.

2

Narrator:

The girl went home and told her father what the widow had said.

3

Daughter:

Father, the widow would like to marry you. She says I will wash in milk every morning and drink wine.

4

Father:

What should I do? Marriage can be a joy, but it can also be miserable. Well, I'll decide another way. Here, daughter, see this boot with the hole in it? Take it up to the attic, hang it on a nail, and pour water into it. If the water stays in it, I'll marry the widow. If it runs out, I won't.

5

Narrator:

The girl did as she was told. When she poured the water into the boot, the leather swelled and the water stayed in the boot.

6

Daughter:

Father, the boot held the water.

7

Father:

Let me see for myself, Daughter.

8

From *Scary Readers Theatre*. © 1994 Suzanne I. Barchers. Teacher Ideas Press. P.O. Box 6633, Englewood, CO 80155. 1-800-237-6124.

Narrator:
When the man saw it was true, he went to the widow and began courting her. 9
The morning after the wedding, the two girls got up, and the husband's daughter
had milk to wash in and wine to drink. The wife's daughter had water to wash
in and water to drink. But the next morning, both girls had water to wash in and
water to drink. And on the third morning, the husband's daughter had water to
wash in and water to drink, while her stepsister got the milk and wine. Because
the stepmother hated her stepdaughter for her beauty and kindness, it continued
like that until one cold winter day.

Stepmother:
Stepdaughter, come and put on this paper dress. Go out into the woods and find 10
a basket of strawberries. I find myself craving something sweet and juicy.

Daughter:
But strawberries don't grow in the winter, and everything is covered with snow. 11
Besides, this paper dress can't possibly keep me warm enough. I'll freeze in
this weather.

Stepmother:
Don't talk back to me. Be off with you, and don't show your face until that 12
basket is filled with strawberries. Here is a piece of bread that will last you for
the day.

Narrator:
The stepmother thought that she could be rid of her stepdaughter, because the 13
girl would surely freeze. The girl obediently put on the paper dress and went
out into the freezing cold. She wandered along, looking for some signs of life,
but not even a blade of grass was showing. After a while, she came to a hut in
the woods. Three dwarfs peered out at her.

Daughter:
Good morning, kind gentlemen. 14

Three Dwarfs:
Come in! Come in out of the cold! 15

Narrator:
The girl sat down by the stove to warm herself and took out her bread. 16

From *Scary Readers Theatre.* © 1994 Suzanne I. Barchers. Teacher Ideas Press. P.O. Box 6633, Englewood, CO 80155. 1-800-237-6124.

Three Dwarfs:
Here, give us some of that bread! 17

Daughter:
Of course. Here is half of all I have. 18

First Dwarf:
What are you doing out in the dead of winter in that paper dress? 19

Daughter:
I've been sent to pick a basketful of strawberries, but it is too cold and snowy 20
for anything to grow.

Second Dwarf:
Here is a broom. Sweep the snow from the back door. 21

Narrator:
While she swept the back stoop, the three dwarfs talked among themselves. 22

Third Dwarf:
What shall we do? She was so cold and had so little, yet she shared her bread 23
with us.

First Dwarf:
I shall give her a gift. She shall become more beautiful each and every day. 24

Second Dwarf:
My gift is that whenever she says a word, a gold piece shall fall from her mouth. 25

Third Dwarf:
My gift is that a king shall choose her for his wife. 26

Narrator:
Meanwhile, as the girl swept, she uncovered a patch of ripe strawberies. She 27
filled her basket and returned inside the hut.

Daughter:
Thank you, kind sirs. I now can return home safely. You have been so good to me. 28

Narrator:
The girl ran home. As she told her story, gold pieces fell from her mouth. 29

Daughter:
> You would not believe what has happened to me. I walked through the woods   30
> to a hut where three dwarfs live. While I was there, I found these strawberries.

Narrator:
> By this time, the floor was covered with gold pieces. Her stepsister saw the gold   31
> and wanted some for herself.

Stepsister:
> Mother, I want to go to the dwarfs' hut so I can have all that gold.   32

Stepmother:
> No, my dear. It is much too cold, and you'll freeze.   33

Stepsister:
> That isn't fair, Mother. Why should she have all the gold? I have to go too.   34

Narrator:
> Finally, the stepmother made her daughter a beautiful fur coat and gave her a   35
> basket of sandwiches and cake to take along. When she got to the hut, the
> stepdaughter ignored the dwarfs, went right in, sat herself down, and began to
> eat her sandwiches and cake.

First Dwarf:
> Here, miss, share some with us.   36

Stepsister:
> Ha! I hardly have enough for myself!   37

Second Dwarf:
> Then take this broom and sweep around the back door.   38

Stepsister:
> Phooey! Go and do your own sweeping. I'm not your maid.   39

Narrator:
> Soon the stepsister became bored waiting for the dwarfs to give her gifts and   40
> went outside. While she was out, they talked together.

Third Dwarf:
> What shall we give this horrid girl?   41

From *Scary Readers Theatre*. © 1994 Suzanne I. Barchers. Teacher Ideas Press. P.O. Box 6633, Englewood, CO 80155. 1-800-237-6124.

First Dwarf:

My gift is that she shall become uglier each and every day. 42

Second Dwarf:

My gift is that whenever she says a word, a toad shall jump out of her mouth. 43

Third Dwarf:

And my gift is that of a horrible death. 44

Narrator:

The girl didn't find any strawberries outside and went angrily home. Meanwhile, the stepmother was growing enraged at her stepdaughter's beauty. She took a kettle and boiled yarn in it. She threw the yarn over her stepdaughter's shoulder, sent her outside with an ax, and told her to go cut a hole in the ice of the river and rinse the yarn in it. While the girl was chopping at the ice, a king in a marvelous carriage came along. 45

King:

Who are you, my dear? And what are you doing? 46

Daughter:

I'm just a poor girl who is rinsing this yarn. 47

King:

Would you like to go away with me? 48

Daughter:

Oh yes, I would gladly go with you. 49

Narrator:

She rode away with the king, and they soon married. A year later, the young queen gave birth to a son. When her stepmother heard of her good fortune, she and her daughter came to the palace as if to pay their respects. Once the king had left for the day, they grabbed the queen and threw her out the window. The ugly stepsister lay down in the bed, pretending to be the queen. Soon the king returned, intending to speak to his wife. 50

Stepmother:

Not now, my king. She is feeling poorly today and is resting. 51

From *Scary Readers Theatre*. © 1994 Suzanne I. Barchers. Teacher Ideas Press. P.O. Box 6633, Englewood, CO 80155. 1-800-237-6124.

Narrator:

The king came back the next morning and spoke to the ugly stepsister thinking she was his wife. But every time she answered him, a toad jumped from her mouth. Because he was used to gold pieces issuing forth, he asked the stepmother what was wrong with his wife.   52

Stepmother:

Don't you worry. She'll soon be fine again.   53

Narrator:

That night, the kitchen boy was looking out the window and saw a duck swimming in the rivelet. To his surprise, the duck spoke to him.   54

Duck:

What is the king doing? Is he awake or asleep?   55

Narrator:

The boy was too shocked to answer, so the duck spoke again.   56

Duck:

And my guests, what are they doing?   57

Kitchen Boy:

They are all asleep.   58

Duck:

And the sweet baby? Does he sleep as well?   59

Kitchen Boy:

Yes, he sleeps soundly in his cradle.   60

Narrator:

Then the duck became the queen again, went upstairs to the nursery, fed her baby, and covered it with blankets. Soon she turned back into a duck and swam away. The next night, she did the same, but the third night she spoke again to the kitchen boy.   61

Duck:

Go tell the king to stand on the threshold and swing his sword over my head three times.   62

From *Scary Readers Theatre.* © 1994 Suzanne I. Barchers. Teacher Ideas Press. P.O. Box 6633, Englewood, CO 80155. 1-800-237-6124.

Narrator:

The king did as the kitchen boy said, and there stood his wife as alive and lovely as ever. The queen told him all that had happened, and the king hid her while he sent for the stepmother. 63

King:

Tell me, old woman. What should be done to a person who throws someone into the river? 64

Stepmother:

Why, the villain should be shut up in a barrel studded with nails, rolled down the hill, and thrown into the river. 65

King:

Then that is your sentence! 66

Narrator:

And the king sent for just such a barrel, put the stepmother and her daughter in it, hammered the lid on tight, and rolled them down the hill into the ice-cold river. 67

The Tinderbox

SUMMARY

In this story by Hans Christian Andersen, a soldier returns from the war and agrees to help a witch retrieve a magic tinderbox hidden in a tree full of riches. The soldier kills the witch and uses the tinderbox for his own needs. He falls in love with a princess and is nearly hanged, but is rescued by the magic tinderbox.

Reading level: 3.

PRESENTATION SUGGESTIONS

There are a variety of parts, but the narrator and soldier have the longest readings. Consider having the witch exit after her role and having the other small roles enter as needed.

PROPS

These roles lend themselves well to dressing for the script. Props could include a backpack, a plastic sword, a black hat, a dog collar, a drawing of a tree, a tinderbox, and a rope.

CHARACTERS

Narrator

Witch

Soldier

Townsperson

Dog

Princess

Queen

King

Lady-in-Waiting

The Tinderbox

Narrator:

A soldier came marching down the road. He had been in the war and was on his way home. He wore his pack on his back and his sword at his side. He marched left, right, left, right. As he marched, he passed a witch.

1

Witch:

Good evening, young man. I see that you are a soldier with your sword and backpack. How would you like to have all the money you want?

2

Soldier:

Yes, I would be pleased to have lots of money. Thank you.

3

Witch:

See that big tree? Climb to the top of it and slide down into its hollow trunk. I'll tie a rope around you so I can pull you out again.

4

Soldier:

But what will I do down there?

5

Witch:

You will see a large hall with many lamps burning. There will be three doors with keys in the locks. Open the first door. On a chest will be a dog with eyes as big as saucers. Take my apron and spread it on the floor. Put the dog on it, and it won't bother you again. Open the chest, and take as many copper coins as you wish. For silver, go into the next room. Put the dog with eyes as big as plates on my apron, and you can take silver from the chest. If you prefer gold, go into the third room. Put the dog with eyes as big as platters on the apron, and you can take as much gold as you want.

6

Soldier:

But I don't understand. What am I to do for you? You must want something.

7

Witch:

There is only one thing I want: an old tinderbox that my grandmother left the last time she was down there.

8

Soldier:

That is no problem. Tie the rope around my waist, and let's begin.

9

From *Scary Readers Theatre.* © 1994 Suzanne I. Barchers. Teacher Ideas Press. P.O. Box 6633, Englewood, CO 80155. 1-800-237-6124.

Narrator:

The witch tied the rope around the soldier's waist.   10

Witch:

You are tied tight. Take my apron and be careful.   11

Narrator:

The soldier climbed the tree, went down the trunk, and found the room with the   12
burning lamps. He unlocked the first door. He saw a big dog with eyes as big
as saucers sitting on a chest.

Soldier:

Good day to you, dog.   13

Narrator:

He put the dog on the apron, filled his pockets with copper coins, closed the   14
chest, and put the dog back on it. He went to the second room. He saw an even
bigger dog, with eyes as big as plates sitting on a chest.

Soldier:

Another fine dog! Don't worry, I won't bother you.   15

Narrator:

He put the dog on the apron as before. When he saw the silver coins, he emptied   16
his pockets of the copper coins. He filled his pockets and backpack with the
silver coins, closed the chest, put the dog back, and left the room. Then he went
in the third room. The dog sitting on the chest in this room was huge, with eyes
as big as platters. The soldier moved carefully and quietly.

Soldier:

Aren't you the handsome dog!   17

Narrator:

He took off his cap and stared at the dog in fear. Because the apron had worked   18
before, he set the dog on the apron and opened the chest.

Soldier:

My goodness! Look at all that gold!   19

Narrator:

He emptied his pockets and backpack of the silver and filled them with gold. 20
He even filled his boots and cap. He returned the dog to the chest and called up
to the witch.

Soldier:

Pull me up now. I am ready. 21

Witch:

Do you have my tinderbox? 22

Soldier:

You're right. I have forgotten it. I'll get it. 23

Narrator:

He found the tinderbox, and the witch pulled him up. 24

Soldier:

Why do you want the tinderbox? 25

Witch:

That's not your concern. You have your money. Give me my tinderbox. 26

Narrator:

The soldier was feeling courageous with his newfound wealth. 27

Soldier:

Tell me why you want the tinderbox, or I will cut your head off with my sword. 28

Witch:

No! Mind your own business. 29

Narrator:

The soldier drew his sword and cut off her head. He bundled his gold in her 30
apron, and set off to town.

When he came to an inn, he stayed in the finest room, ate the best food,
and purchased the finest clothes. People were happy to tell him about the town
and the king's lovely daughter.

Soldier:

I would like to see her. 31

Townsperson:

    No one sees her. She lives in a castle surrounded by walls and a moat. A fortune   32
teller said she would marry a common soldier, and the king is determined that
this will not happen.

Narrator:

    The soldier thought this was all very interesting and still hoped to meet the   33
king's daughter. He continued to live in a fine manner until he had only two
coins left. He had to move into a tiny room at the top of the inn where it was
very dark. One night, he remembered there was a candle in the tinderbox. He
took it out and struck the flint once on the tinderbox. Suddenly, the dog with
eyes as big as saucers came through the door.

Dog:

    What do you command me to do, Master?   34

Soldier:

    What is this! Is this tinderbox magic? Let's put it to the test. Dog, bring me   35
some money.

Narrator:

    In a flash the dog was back with a sack of copper coins in his mouth.   36

Dog:

    Here is your money, sir.   37

Soldier:

    Why, thank you! This is a fine turn of events. Let's see what happens if I strike   38
the tinderbox twice.

Narrator:

    The soldier discovered that striking the tinderbox twice brought him the dog   39
with eyes as big as plates. This dog brought him a sack of silver coins. Three
strikes brought the dog with eyes as big as platters carrying a bag of gold. Soon
the soldier was living the rich life again. But he wasn't completely content. He
began to think about the princess. He took his tinderbox and struck the flint to
it.

Soldier:

    I would like to see the princess, if only for a minute. Please bring her to me.   40

Dog:

I can do that.   41

Narrator:

The dog with eyes as big as saucers brought the sleeping princess on his back.   42
The soldier fell instantly in love with her and kissed her as she slept. Then the
dog took her home. The next morning, the princess was having breakfast with
the king and queen.

Princess:

I had the strangest dream last night.   43

Queen:

What was that, dear?   44

Princess:

I dreamed that a dog came to my room and carried me away. There was a soldier   45
in a fine room who kissed me.

King:

Just a dream, my dear.   46

Narrator:

But the queen was worried and sent a lady-in-waiting to watch over the princess   47
while she slept. Sure enough, the soldier sent the dog again, but this time the
lady-in-waiting raced after the dog. When she saw where the dog took the
princess, she marked a cross on the door with a piece of chalk.

Lady-in-Waiting:

Now we can get to the bottom of this in the morning.   48

Narrator:

But when the dog returned, it saw the white cross on the door. It took a piece   49
of chalk and marked all the houses in the town. The next morning, the king,
queen, and lady-in-waiting came to the first house.

Lady-in-Waiting:

Here it is!   50

Queen:

No, here it is!   51

King: 52
  No, this must be it!

Narrator: 53
  Everywhere they looked was a house with a white cross on the door. They soon
  gave up, but the clever queen thought of a plan. She sewed a little bag filled
  with buckwheat and tied it around the princess's waist. Then she cut a tiny hole
  in the bag so that the grains fell out one at a time. When the dog took the princess
  the next night, it didn't notice the tiny trail of buckwheat. In the morning, the
  king and queen easily found the soldier. They had him arrested immediately.

Soldier: 54
  What a fix I am in. I love the princess so much. Yet, tomorrow I am to be hanged.

Narrator: 55
  Early the next morning, the townspeople were gathering for the hanging. A boy
  was running by the soldier's window.

Soldier: 56
  Boy! Wait a minute! There won't be a hanging until they come for me. Would you
  take a minute and run to my room in the inn and fetch me my tinderbox? There will
  be four copper coins for you if you do. You have plenty of time before the hanging.

Narrator: 57
  The boy had never had even one coin, let alone four. He ran for the tinderbox and
  brought it to the soldier. Soon, the soldier was delivered to the gallows. As is the
  custom, he asked if he could have one last request. His request was to be allowed to
  smoke a pipe of tobacco. The king couldn't refuse. The soldier struck the tinderbox
  once, then two times, and then three times. The three dogs stood before him.

Soldier: 58
  Help me, dogs. I don't want to hang!

Narrator: 59
  The dogs began to rip and tear at the guards. The dog with eyes as big as platters
  threw the king and queen high into the air. The guards and people shouted for
  the soldier to be their king. He called off the dogs and rode in the carriage back
  to the castle.
  The soldier called out the princess and asked her to be his wife. She agreed
  that marrying the soldier would suit her very well. They had a fine wedding and
  a feast that lasted a week. Of course, the dogs were the guests of honor at the
  table and every meal thereafter.

From *Scary Readers Theatre*. © 1994 Suzanne I. Barchers. Teacher Ideas Press. P.O. Box 6633, Englewood, CO 80155. 1-800-237-6124.

The Voice of Death

SUMMARY

In this Romanian tale, a rich man is determined to escape death. He moves his family to a town where instead of dying, people answer a calling voice and leave. He decides that all he must do is refuse to answer the voice. Then it calls to him.

Reading level: 3.

PRESENTATION SUGGESTIONS

The narrator and the rich man are the main characters and should be near the front. The young man and wife could exit after their lines. The barber could be to the side or enter for his lines.

PROPS

The stage could include shaving equipment by a chair or a table for inside a house. A mural showing a cliff in the background could be included.

CHARACTERS

Narrator

Rich Man

Young Man

Wife

Barber

The Voice of Death

Narrator:
Once there was a man who wanted to be rich. He thought of nothing else and   1
eventually became quite wealthy. Then he decided it would be terrible to die
and lose all his great wealth, so he set out to find a land where no one died.
Whenever he came to a new country, he asked if people died there. When he
was told people did indeed die, he set off for another country. Finally, he came
to a new country where he met a pleasant young man.

Rich Man:
Good morning, sir. This is lovely country. Tell me, does anyone die here?   2

Young Man:
No, sir. We have no death here.   3

Rich Man:
But how can that be? Don't you have great numbers of people in your land?   4

Young Man:
No. You see, from time to time a voice is heard calling to one person or another.   5
When people hear that voice, they go away, never to return.

Rich Man:
Do they see this person who is calling or just hear the voice?   6

Young Man:
They seem to see and hear whoever calls.   7

Narrator:
The man couldn't believe that people were foolish enough to follow the voice   8
knowing they would never return. He decided he would gather his wife and
family and move all his possessions to this wonderful country. He would see
to it that no one in his family ever followed that voice, no matter what it said.
Soon, he was settled in his new home.

Rich Man:
Dear family, I have gathered you together because it is very important that if a   9
voice calls to you it must be ignored. Otherwise, you will go to your death.

Wife:
I don't understand. How could a voice cause our death?   10

From *Scary Readers Theatre.* © 1994 Suzanne I. Barchers. Teacher Ideas Press. P.O. Box 6633, Englewood, CO 80155. 1-800-237-6124.

Rich Man:

All I can say is that you must never follow any unknown voice that calls to you. Promise me this.   11

Narrator:

The family promised, and they enjoyed many good years. But one day, when they were sitting around the table, the man's wife suddenly jumped up.   12

Wife: *(Loudly)*

I'm coming! I'm coming!   13

Rich Man: *(Firmly)*

Don't you remember what I told you? Don't answer that voice or you will die. Stay where you are!   14

Wife:

But it's calling to me. Can't you hear it? I'll just go and see what it wants and come right back. Don't worry. I promise I'll be right back!   15

Narrator:

Her husband tried to stop her, but she fought to get away. He shut and barred all his doors.   16

Wife:

All right, husband, I'll obey you and stay right here.   17

Narrator:

But a few minutes later, she dashed for one of the doors. Her husband caught her by her coat.   18

Rich Man: *(Pleading)*

Please, my dear wife, don't go, or you will never return.   19

Narrator:

But his wife slipped out of her coat and ran away.   20

Wife:

I'm coming! I'm coming!   21

Rich Man: *(Sadly)*

I warned her, but I see I can't stop her. I shall miss her dearly.   22

Narrator:
Years passed, and the rich man lived peacefully. One day, he was at the barber's   23
getting shaved. Suddenly, he sat up in the chair.

Rich Man: *(Loudly)*
I won't come. Hear me? I won't come!   24

Barber:
What is wrong with you? Why are you shouting like that?   25

Rich Man: *(Still louder)*
I'm telling you, I won't come, so just go away.   26

Barber:
Sir, please. You are upsetting everyone. Sit back and let me finish your shave.   27

Rich Man: *(Even louder)*
Go away! Call as much as you want, but I will have no part of this. You'll never   28
get me to come.

Narrator:
The rich man suddenly stood up and grabbed the barber's razor.   29

Rich Man:
Give me that razor! I'll show you to leave me alone when I say so!   30

Narrator:
With that, he ran out of the shop, chasing someone no one else could see. The   31
barber wanted his razor, so he chased after the man. When they got well out of
town, the man dropped the razor, fell off a cliff, and was never seen again. The
barber went home with his razor and spoke to the townspeople.

Barber:
Listen everyone. I have found where everyone goes when they hear the voice and   32
leave this country. They have all fallen off the cliff into a pit. Come. I'll show you.

Narrator:
But when the people went to examine the pit, they found that it wasn't full of   33
all the people who had left the country. It was empty. But from that time on,
when people became old or sick, they died just like other people in the world.

From *Scary Readers Theatre*. © 1994 Suzanne I. Barchers. Teacher Ideas Press. P.O. Box 6633, Englewood, CO 80155. 1-800-237-6124.

The Witches with the Horns

SUMMARY

In this Irish tale, twelve horned witches come to a woman's house, disturbing her quiet evening and threatening her family. With some help from the Spirit of the Well, she tricks the witches into leaving and prevents their return.
Reading level: 3.

PRESENTATION SUGGESTIONS

The narrator should stand to one side. The woman should be nearby, with the witches arranged across the stage or entering as each speaks. The spirit of the well, feet-water, and cake can be toward the back.

PROPS

Items could be used that look as though they are from an old-fashioned kitchen or living room: a table, rocking chair, dishes, and so forth. Skeins of wool or a spinning wheel would add interest to the stage.

CHARACTERS

Narrator

Woman

Witch with One Horn

Witch with Two Horns

Witch with Three Horns

Spirit of the Well

Feet-water

Cake

Door

The Witches with the Horns

Narrator:
　One night, a wealthy woman was enjoying a quiet evening, carding her wool　　1
while her family slept. Suddenly, her peace was interrupted by a loud knock at
the door.

Woman:
　Who is there? *(Pause)* Please, who is there?　　2

Narrator:
　The woman assumed it was a neighbor and went to the door. To her surprise,　　3
in came a woman with a horn on her forehead. She was clearly a witch. She sat
down and began to card the wool.

Witch with One Horn:
　Where are the other women? They must be late.　　4

Narrator:
　Again, there was a knock at the door.　　5

Woman: *(Timidly)*
　Who is there?　　6

Witch with One Horn:
　Go and answer the door.　　7

Narrator:
　This time a woman with two horns on her forehead came into the living room.　　8
She carried a spinning wheel.

Witch with Two Horns:
　Good evening. I am the witch of two horns. I am going to set up my spinning　　9
wheel right here by the fire.

Narrator:
　Again and again there was a knock at the door, and each time a witch would　　10
enter. Each witch would have still another horn on her head. Finally there were
twelve witches, the last with twelve horns on her head. They carded, spun, and
weaved, singing ancient rhymes while they worked. The woman could feel their
spell on her, keeping her from calling for help.

From *Scary Readers Theatre*. © 1994 Suzanne I. Barchers. Teacher Ideas Press. P.O. Box 6633, Englewood, CO 80155. 1-800-237-6124.

Witch with Three Horns:

Woman, take this sieve and bring water from the well. Then make us a cake to eat.　　11

Narrator:

The woman took the sieve, but when she got to the well, she wondered how she　　12
could carry water in a sieve.

Woman:

Oh Spirit of the Well, I need your help. How may I carry water in a sieve?　　13

Spirit of the Well:

Use the clay and moss and cover the sieve with it. That will hold the water.　　14

Narrator:

The woman did as the spirit said, but needed more help to rid her house of the　　15
witches.

Woman:

Spirit of the Well, I need your help again. How can I get rid of these witches?　　16
They have taken over my house.

Spirit of the Well:

Here is how you can trick them. Go to the north side of the house. When you　　17
get there, repeat three times, "The mountain of the Fenian Women and the sky
about it is on fire."

Narrator:

The woman of the house was frightened, but she drew on all her courage and　　18
returned to the house. She went to the north side of the house and called out the
message.

Woman: (*Loudly*)

The mountain of the Fenian Women and the sky about it is on fire.　　19

Witches with the Horns: (*Together*)

No! No!　　20

Narrator:

The witches with the horns rushed from the house. The woman immediately　　21
returned to the well to give thanks.

Woman:
Thank you, Spirit of the Well. Your trick worked! The witches all have left.   22

Spirit of the Well:
Don't thank me yet, for they surely will return. Here is what you must do next.   23
Take the water used to wash your children's feet and sprinkle it on the threshold
and down the path. The witches have made a cake using a few drops of blood
from your family, making them helpless. Break that cake into bits and put a
piece in each family member's mouth. Then take the cloth the witches have
woven and put it in your chest. Finally, bar the door against their return.

Narrator:
The woman did all the spirit told her. Soon she heard the witches at her door.   24

Witches with the Horns: *(Together)*
Open, feet-water! Open, feet-water!   25

Feet-water:
I can't open the door. I have been scattered on the threshold and down the path.   26

Witches with the Horns: *(Together)*
Open cake, that we mixed with blood!   27

Cake:
I can't open the door. I have been broken and placed in the mouths of the family.   28

Witches with the Horns: *(Together)*
Open door! Open door!   29

Door:
I can't! The bar is down, and I can't move.   30

Narrator:
The witches swirled around the house three times, looking for an entrance.   31
When they saw they couldn't get in, they left in anger. The woman hung up the
witches' cloth to show she had conquered them. They never bothered her or her
family again.

From *Scary Readers Theatre.* © 1994 Suzanne I. Barchers. Teacher Ideas Press. P.O. Box 6633, Englewood, CO 80155. 1-800-237-6124.

Part 3

Antoine

Antoine

SUMMARY

In this French tale, Antoine's trickery costs three brothers their sheep, their wives, and, finally, their lives.
Reading level: 4

PRESENTATION SUGGESTIONS

The narrator can remain to the front and side throughout the play. Antoine should be near the center. The mother can exit between her parts. The three brothers can remain on stage and to the side once they have entered. The beggar can enter and exit with his lines.

PROPS

A whistle could be used during the mother's death scene. Burlap sacks could be placed on the stage. Antoine, his mother, and the beggar could be dressed poorly, with the brothers in farming clothes.

CHARACTERS

Narrator

Mother

Antoine

Wolf

Oldest Brother

Middle Brother

Youngest Brother

Beggar

Antoine

Narrator:
Once upon a time there lived a widow and her son, Antoine. They were very poor, but instead of going to work, Antoine stood around on the street, staring at the ground. 1

Mother:
Son, come here. I want you to go into the forest and collect enough dry leaves to make beds for us. You are very lazy, but even though you will never catch a wolf by the tail, at least you can do this simple task. 2

Narrator:
Before Antoine finished his chore, it began to rain. He crawled into the hollow trunk of a tree to keep dry and soon fell fast asleep. After some time, he was awakened by a scratching sound, and looking out, he saw a wolf. He hid in the back of the tree while the wolf came in. Then he suddenly remembered that his mother once told him that a wolf could neither bend his back nor turn his head to look behind him. He grabbed the wolf's tail, pulled it out of the tree, and went home. 3

Antoine:
Mother, you said I would never catch a wolf by the tail, but look at this! 4

Mother:
Sakes alive! What shall we do with him! I know. Fetch the skin of the ram that died last week, and we will sew the wolf up in it. He will make a splendid ram, and tomorrow we can sell him at the fair. 5

Wolf: *(Thinking aloud)*
I may as well go along with them. I can always get away later. 6

Narrator:
The next day, many farmers bid on the magnificent ram, but he was finally bought by three brothers. 7

Oldest Brother:
Brothers, because my flock is nearest, I will take him home to my sheepfold tonight, and, later, we can decide what pasture would be best. 8

From *Scary Readers Theatre*. © 1994 Suzanne I. Barchers. Teacher Ideas Press. P.O. Box 6633, Englewood, CO 80155. 1-800-237-6124.

Wolf: *(Thinking aloud)*

    Ah, this might not be so bad after all.   9

Narrator:

    The next morning, the young farmer rose early and went immediately to his   10
sheepfold. To his dismay, he found the sheep were all dead except one that had
been completely devoured. The wolf pretended to be asleep in the corner.

Oldest Brother:

    This is no ordinary ram, but at least I can pay back my brother for tricking me   11
last year.

Narrator:

    And so the oldest brother took the beast to the middle brother, telling him the   12
ram wouldn't eat his grass.

Middle Brother:

    I'll take him to my pasture right away. Perhaps the grass there will suit him   13
better.

Narrator:

    The next morning, the middle brother discovered all his sheep dead and took   14
the ram to his youngest brother. Soon his sheep were dead as well. The brothers
then gathered together and decided to take the beast back to Antoine. As they
approached Antoine's house, he saw them coming and ran inside.

Antoine: *(Shouting)*

    Mother, Mother! The men are bringing the wolf back. Surely they have found   15
out the truth and will want to kill me, and maybe you as well.

Mother:

    This is a disaster. What shall we do?   16

Antoine:

    Quick! Do just as I say. Lie down on the floor and pretend to be dead. Don't   17
move or speak, no matter what happens.

Narrator:

    When the brothers entered the hut, they found the widow lying on the floor and   18
Antoine blowing a whistle into her ear.

Oldest Brother:
What are you doing now, Antoine?

19

Antoine:
Oh, my friends, I am so miserable. I have just lost my dear mother. I don't know what will happen to me now.

20

Youngest Brother:
Why are you blowing that shrill whistle?

21

Antoine:
This is my only chance! This whistle has been known to bring the dead to life. I had hoped it would work and bring my dear mother back to me.
Look! I think she moved. Yes, yes! Look, her nostrils are moving. And see, her hands are twitching.

22

Narrator:
Antoine blew the whistle again, and soon the widow was able to lift her head.

23

Youngest Brother:
Look, we know you are a trickster and a cheat. You sold us a ram, knowing it was a wolf.

24

Middle Brother:
That's right. It destroyed all our sheep and we came here to pay you back.

25

Oldest Brother:
But . . . if you will give us that whistle, we will forget your trickery and leave.

26

Antoine: (*Hesitating*)
Well, this is my only treasure, but I guess I have no choice.

27

Narrator:
The brothers left with the whistle, talking as they walked.

28

Youngest Brother:
I have an idea! Let's teach our lazy wives a good lesson.

29

Middle Brother:
Ahh, we think alike. Let's kill our wives, giving them a good fright. And then we can restore them to life again.

30

From *Scary Readers Theatre*. © 1994 Suzanne I. Barchers. Teacher Ideas Press. P.O. Box 6633, Englewood, CO 80155. 1-800-237-6124.

Oldest Brother:

    What a clever plan. I wouldn't have thought of that.   31

Narrator:

    The men found their wives cooking together and immediately knocked each   32
down, killing all three. Then each brother tried the whistle, blowing so loudly
their lungs ached, but the wives only turned cold as stone. Slowly, the brothers
realized they had been tricked again. They took a large sack and returned to
Antoine's hut.

Youngest Brother:

    Here he is, sound asleep. Throw him in the sack and tie it tightly. Let's go to   33
the river.

Narrator:

    But it was a long way to the river, and soon they tired of carrying him. Seeing   34
an inn, they decided to leave him outside while they refreshed themselves. The
brothers failed to notice an old beggar sitting nearby, but Antoine heard him
eating and began to moan softly.

Antoine:

    Ahhh, ohhh.   35

Beggar:

    What is this? Why are you tied in that sack?   36

Antoine:

    They want to make me a bishop, and I would not agree.   37

Beggar:

    But that isn't such a bad thing.   38

Antoine:

    Perhaps not, but I would hate it. If you think it would be so great, why don't   39
you take my place?

Beggar:

    Why, I think I will do exactly that!   40

From *Scary Readers Theatre.* © 1994 Suzanne I. Barchers. Teacher Ideas Press. P.O. Box 6633, Englewood, CO 80155. 1-800-237-6124.

Narrator:
And so the beggar untied the sack, climbed in, and soon was thrown into the river to drown.   41

The next morning, the brothers buried their wives, and as they returned from the cemetery they met Antoine, driving a great herd of sheep. The brothers were astonished.

Oldest Brother:
You! You scoundrel!   42

Middle Brother:
You should be drowned! What are you doing here?   43

Antoine:
Didn't you know? Beneath this world is another one that is far richer. That is where I went when you flung me into the river. It happened that I was close to a sheep fair, so I took these sheep which were free for the taking. If only I had landed by the horse fair, I would be much the richer for it.   44

Youngest Brother:
Do you know where that spot in the river is?   45

Antoine:
Of course, for I saw it with my own eyes.   46

Oldest Brother:
Well, if you don't want us to avenge our dead sheep and murdered wives, you will throw us into the river at that very spot.   47

Antoine:
Very well, but I will need three sacks so I can throw each of you in.   48

Narrator:
And so Antoine threw each of them in, and they were never seen again. To this day, no one knows if they landed near the horse fair.   49

The Creature Who Came to Dinner

SUMMARY

In this Russian tale, a dragon disrupts a feast the czar is giving. Vladimir taunts the dragon, provoking a fight and outwitting the beast.

Reading level: 4.

PRESENTATION SUGGESTIONS

The characters can be arranged across the stage in their speaking order and remain onstage throughout the play.

PROPS

Props might include Russian artifacts, a wine bottle or carafe, a sword, and a table with cutlery and plates.

CHARACTERS

Narrator

Vladimir

Dragon

Czar

Czarina

SCARIER!!

The Creature Who Came to Dinner

Narrator:
The czar was giving a fine feast for many noblemen and noblewomen. Everyone was enjoying their food and drink when, suddenly, a huge dragon with teeth like spikes and claws like spears sneaked into the hall. He roared at the guests, and flames and smoke shot out of his mouth. The ugly beast lumbered over to the head table and pushed his way between the czar and his wife, the czarina. One of the guests, Vladimir, spoke up.

1

Vladimir:
Have you no manners? What kind of beast are you to disturb the czar's feast?

2

Narrator:
The beast simply reared back its bold head and roared at the guests.

3

Dragon: *(Loudly)*
Bring me meat! Now!

4

Czar: *(Clapping hands)*
Come! Come! Bring us the roast!

5

Narrator:
The servants brought out a huge roast, but before anyone could carve it, the dragon scooped it up and swallowed it whole.

6

Vladimir:
You are a dreadful beast, and you have absolutely no manners.

7

Dragon: *(Loudly)*
Bring me wine! Now!

8

Czar: *(Clapping hands)*
Bring the wine! Quickly now!

9

Narrator:
When the wine came, the dragon grabbed it and drank it down in a single swallow.

10

From *Scary Readers Theatre*. © 1994 Suzanne I. Barchers. Teacher Ideas Press. P.O. Box 6633, Englewood, CO 80155. 1-800-237-6124.

Vladimir:

You are not only a beast, but you are also a glutton. I hope you drink so much
wine you burst!

11

Dragon: *(Loudly)*

Now you have made me angry! Come outside so we can fight!

12

Vladimir:

Gladly!

13

Narrator:

The dragon and Vladimir rose to leave the room. The czarina stopped Vladimir.

14

Czarina:

Why did you provoke him, Vladimir? It would have been better to feed him and
let him go. Now you have to fight him. You very well may be killed.

15

Vladimir:

Don't worry, your highness. Everything will be fine.

16

Narrator:

Everyone in the party followed Vladimir and the dragon outside. The people
were discussing who would win the battle, and they watched the two combatants
excitedly.

17

Dragon:

Well, Vladimir, I hope you are ready to die! I think I will chew you to death
with my sharp teeth. No, I think I'll use my claws first to cut you into tiny little
pieces. Actually, I like my meat cooked. So I think I'll burn you with my breath,
and then I'll cut you up into bite-sized chunks.

18

Vladimir:

Wait just a minute, dragon. I agreed to fight you, but I didn't agree to fight your
whole army!

19

Dragon:

What are you talking about? I didn't bring any army.

20

Vladimir:

Then what is that over there?

21

From *Scary Readers Theatre.* © 1994 Suzanne I. Barchers. Teacher Ideas Press. P.O. Box 6633, Englewood, CO 80155. 1-800-237-6124.

Narrator:
> The dragon, being not especially smart, turned to see what Vladimir was talking about. As soon the dragon turned away, Vladimir drew his sword and cut off the monster's head.

22

Vladimir:
> Well, my friends, the fight is over. Let us return to the table and finish this wonderful meal.

23

Narrator:
> And that was the end of the creature who came to dinner.

24

The Fiddler's Contest

SUMMARY

In this American tale, when Dukedom has a fiddling contest to raise money for a new jail wall, everyone hopes Ples Haslock will fiddle, even though he has been ailing. When he shows up, everyone expects that he'll win, but no one expects the finale to the contest. This could be paired with "Aaron Kelly's Bones."
Reading level: 4.

PRESENTATION SUGGESTIONS

The narrator, county clerk, Coot, and Ples could be arranged across one side of the stage with the townspeople, judge, and doctor entering for their lines and remaining on stage through the end of the play.

PROPS

A variety of violins could be placed on the stage. The background could include murals of the jail, the swamp, Ples's shack, or a crowd listening to a fiddler.

CHARACTERS

Narrator

County Clerk

Coot Kersey

Ples Haslock

First Townsperson

Second Townsperson

Judge

Doctor

The Fiddler's Contest

Narrator:
There was never a better fiddler than Ples Haslock. He fiddled for all the square 1
dances and parties around the countryside. Not only was he the best fiddler, he
was also as handsome as could be. But Ples had no use for the girls. He only
wanted to play that fiddle.

Once, the wall of the jail in Dukedom fell out, and because there was no
money to fix it, the city folk decided to have a fiddling contest to raise the
money.

County Clerk:
We'll have to send over and tell Ples about the contest. 2

Coot Kersey:
I don't know if he'll be able to come this year. I hear he has heart dropsy. 3

County Clerk:
Coot, you're just *hoping* he won't show up so you'll have a chance at winning 4
the fiddling contest for a change.

Narrator:
The county clerk went over to Ples's shack and knocked on the door. 5

Ples Haslock:
Who's there? 6

County Clerk:
Just me, Ples. 7

Ples Haslock:
Come on in then. How you doing? Haven't seen you since I don't know when! 8
How's everything in Dukedom?

County Clerk:
Can't complain, Ples, can't complain. 9

Narrator:
The county clerk was shocked at how bad Ples looked. He had lost an awful lot 10
of weight, but his eyes were as bright blue as ever.

County Clerk:

How're you feeling, Ples?   11

Ples Haslock:

Well, I could say I was pretty down, but my good neighbor women bring me   12
something to eat each day, and the men make sure I don't fall out of bed at
night. Other times, I just lay around and play my fiddle. Heart dropsy seems to
run in the family, but I aim to be up and around soon.

County Clerk:

Well, I don't know if you'll be up to it, but we're having a fiddling contest to   13
raise money for fixing the jail. It'll be at the Dukedom school in two weeks,
but maybe you shouldn't worry yourself about it.

Ples Haslock:

What do you mean, worry myself! Why, you can count on me! I'll be there for   14
sure!

County Clerk:

Well, I know everyone will be mighty glad to hear that. Now I better be on my   15
way. We'll be looking for you in two weeks then.

Narrator:

The night of the contest came, and everyone was excited for the festivities to   16
start. The judge came out and read off the names of the seven contestants, but
the list didn't include Ples.

First Townsperson:

Where's Ples?   17

Second Townsperson:

We can't have a fiddling contest without Ples!   18

Judge:

Now I know you're disappointed that Ples hasn't shown up, but he's been laid   19
up in bed lately. I reckon he couldn't make the trip over here. We'll just have
to go on without him.

From *Scary Readers Theatre*. © 1994 Suzanne I. Barchers. Teacher Ideas Press. P.O. Box 6633, Englewood, CO 80155. 1-800-237-6124.

Narrator:
The crowd grumbled a bit but settled down to hear the fiddlers. Five of them shouldn't have even bothered to enter the contest with their sorry sawing. Coot and Old Rob were the best, even though watching Coot was like watching a turkey gobbler bobbing around. His playing was right powerful, though, and the crowd clapped along with the music. When Old Rob played, the crowd went plumb wild, stamping and shouting at his energetic playing. It was pretty clear that Old Rob would be the winner.

But before Old Rob could be declared the winner, the crowd suddenly heard another fiddler. There was Ples, pale and sickly looking, but fiddling better than ever. He played for an hour, and when he finished, the crowd was ready to tear down the place with their whooping and hollering.

20

Judge:
Quiet my friends, quiet! It's clear we have a winner! I hearby present this prize to Ples Haslock for his fine fiddling.

21

Narrator:
Ples stood up holding his fiddle and bow under his left arm, but then he crashed to the ground.

22

Judge: *(Shouting)*
Get a doctor! I can't feel a heartbeat!

23

Second Townsperson:
Poor Ples! He came all this way just to win a contest with his last breath.

24

First Townsperson:
He sure did like to fiddle!

25

Second Townsperson:
Look at his clothes, all covered with clay. Looks like he walked through the swamp on his way here.

26

Narrator:
The doctor finally arrived and looked over poor Ples.

27

Doctor:
How'd he get here?

28

Judge:

He played in the contest and then just keeled over dead right before our eyes.　29

Doctor:

This man didn't just keel over. He's been dead for at least forty-eight hours.　30
And from the clay on his clothes, I'd say he's been buried, too!

Narrator:

Some of the townfolk returned with the doctor to bury old Ples again, and the　31
jail got a new wall. But it was a long time before there was another fiddling
contest in Dukedom.

Fowler's Fowl

SUMMARY

In this German tale adapted from the Brothers Grimm, a wizard tricks three sisters into coming into his house, killing the first two. The third sister rescues the others, restores them to life, and escapes. Her family exacts their revenge.

Reading level: 4.

PRESENTATION SUGGESTIONS

The narrator has a major role and should be towards the front of the stage. The wizard and three sisters should be arranged across the stage. The wedding guest could enter and exit near the end of the script.

PROPS

Props might include a basket, an egg, and a set of keys, and the stage could be littered with a few feathers.

CHARACTERS

Narrator

Eldest Sister

Wizard

Middle Sister

Youngest Sister

Wedding Guest

Fowler's Fowl

Narrator:

There once was a wizard who dressed up as a poor man with a basket for handouts and went begging at houses. When a pretty girl opened the door, he captured her, and she never was seen again. One day, he came to the door of a man who had three lovely daughters and knocked on the door.

1

Eldest Sister:

Good morning, sir.

2

Wizard:

Good morning, my dear.

3

Narrator:

And after that short greeting, the wizard leaned forward, touched the girl, and caused her to leap into his basket. He took her to his house, which was quite grand, and he treated her very kindly.

4

Wizard:

My dear, I am sure you'll be quite happy here because you may have whatever your heart desires. Now, I have to go away for a few days. Here are the keys to the house. You may go into any room except the one that this little key opens. You must also take care of this egg. Keep it safe with you at all times. If you defy me, you will die.

5

Eldest Sister:

As you wish, master. I promise I will take care of the keys and the egg.

6

Narrator:

After the wizard left, she looked in room after room, admiring how they glistened with gold and silver. Finally, she came to the forbidden door, and try though she might, she couldn't resist a little peek. She put the key in the lock and turned it just a bit. The door sprang open, and she found a huge tub of dead bodies that had been chopped into bloody pieces. Next to the tub was a block of wood with an axe on it. In her fear, the girl dropped the egg in the tub. When she took it out, she couldn't wipe the blood off. Soon, the wizard returned.

7

Wizard:

Have you obeyed me while I was gone?

8

From *Scary Readers Theatre*. © 1994 Suzanne I. Barchers. Teacher Ideas Press. P.O. Box 6633, Englewood, CO 80155. 1-800-237-6124.

Eldest Sister:
  Of course, Master.   9

Wizard:
  Then let me see the egg.   10

Eldest Sister:
  Please, sir, must I?   11

Narrator:
  He insisted, and she showed him the egg.   12

Wizard:
  You went against my wishes, and now you must die.   13

Narrator:
  He dragged her into the forbidden room, chopped her into pieces, and threw her   14
  into the tub. Then he returned to her house for the middle sister. He knocked at
  the door.

Middle Sister:
  Good morning, sir.   15

Wizard:
  Good morning, my dear.   16

Narrator:
  Once again, he touched her and caused her to leap into his basket. He took her   17
  to his home, and after some time, he called her to him.

Wizard:
  Now, I have to go away for a few days. Here are the keys to the house. You   18
  may go into any room except the one that this little key opens. You must also
  take care of this egg. Keep it safe with you at all times. If you defy me, you
  will die.

Middle Sister:
  As you wish, Master. I promise I will take care of the keys and the egg.   19

From *Scary Readers Theatre*. © 1994 Suzanne I. Barchers. Teacher Ideas Press. P.O. Box 6633, Englewood, CO 80155. 1-800-237-6124.

Narrator:

But once again, curiosity got the better of the girl. When the wizard returned, he found her out, killed her, and returned for the youngest sister. 20

Youngest Sister:

Good morning, sir. 21

Wizard:

Good morning, my dear. 22

Narrator:

Once again, the wizard leaned forward, touched the girl, and caused her to leap into his basket. He took her to his home, and after some time, he called her to him. 23

Wizard:

Now, I have to go away for a few days. Here are the keys to the house. You may go into any room except the one that this little key opens. You must also take care of this egg. Keep it safe with you at all times. If you defy me, you will die. 24

Youngest Sister:

As you wish, Master. I promise I will take care of the keys and the egg. 25

Narrator:

The youngest sister was every bit as curious as her sisters, but before she explored, she put the egg away in a safe place. When she opened the door to the forbidden room and found her dead sisters, she carefully put their body parts into their proper places. When all the pieces were joined, they began to return to life. 26

Youngest Sister:

Thank goodness! You're alive! We must plan how we are going to trick the wizard. 27

Narrator:

The sisters plotted and were ready when the wizard returned. He called for the youngest sister and was pleased when he saw the egg was not stained. 28

Wizard:

Well, my dear, you have passed the test. You shall be my wife. 29

From *Scary Readers Theatre*. © 1994 Suzanne I. Barchers. Teacher Ideas Press. P.O. Box 6633, Englewood, CO 80155. 1-800-237-6124.

Youngest Sister:

Very well, but first you must carry a basket of gold on your back to my mother and father. I will prepare for the wedding while you are gone.　30

Narrator:

The wizard agreed and prepared to go to her house. The youngest sister ran to her sisters, put them in a basket, and covered them with gold.　31

Youngest Sister:

The wizard will carry you back to our parents, but when you get home you must send help for me.　32

Narrator:

The wizard put the basket on his back and bade the youngest sister farewell.　33

Youngest Sister:

Goodbye, Master. Do not tarry or rest, for I will be watching from my window.　34

Narrator:

The wizard started on his way, but the basket became heavy. He stopped, but the eldest sister was ready for him.　35

Eldest Sister:

I'm watching from my window, and I see you resting. Don't stop now.　36

Narrator:

The wizard thought it was his bride-to-be and set off again. Soon he was tired again and paused to catch his breath.　37

Middle Sister:

I'm watching from my window, and I see you resting. Don't stop now.　38

Narrator:

The wizard trudged on, finally delivering the basket to the bride's family. Meanwhile, the bride was preparing for the wedding, inviting all the wizard's friends. She took a skull, decorated it with jewels and flowers, and set it in the attic window looking out. Next she covered herself with honey, split open a feather bed, and rolled in the feathers. She left the house, looking like a strange bird. On her way, she met a wedding guest.　39

Wedding Guest:
Where are you from, fowler's fowl? 40

Youngest Sister:
From Fitz the Fowler's house. 41

Wedding Guest:
What is the bride doing? 42

Youngest Sister:
She has swept the whole house and looks out the attic window for her groom. 43

Narrator:
Soon, she met the wizard who was walking slowly home. 44

Wizard:
Oh fowler's fowl, where are you from? 45

Youngest Sister:
From Fitz the Fowler's house I've come. 46

Wizard:
Tell me what the bride is doing. 47

Youngest Sister:
She swept the whole house and now looks out the attic window for her groom. 48

Narrator:
He looked up, saw the skull in the window, nodded, and waved. When he and his guests were inside, the sisters' brothers and cousins arrived to rescue her. They locked the doors and set fire to the house. The wizard and all his friends burned to death, and young girls never disappeared again. 49

From *Scary Readers Theatre*. © 1994 Suzanne I. Barchers. Teacher Ideas Press. P.O. Box 6633, Englewood, CO 80155. 1-800-237-6124.

The Headless Haunt

SCARIEST!!!

SUMMARY

In this tale from the southern United States, a poor, cold man and his wife help a ghost reunite his head with his body and are richly rewarded.
Reading level: 4.

PRESENTATION SUGGESTIONS

Because there are only four characters, all can share the stage equally.

PROPS

The stage can be set up to look like a kitchen or cellar. Consider including a candlestick, shovel, old fashioned pots and cutlery, firewood, food, and so forth.

CHARACTERS

Narrator

Husband

Haunt

Wife

The Headless Haunt

Narrator:

Once, a man, his wife, and their two children were walking along the road. It was cold, and the road was sticky with mud. Though their feet were nearly frozen and they were terribly hungry, they trudged on until they came to a deserted log cabin with a fire in the fireplace and light in the windows. The travellers didn't know that the man who owned it had been killed by robbers. 1

Husband:

Let's go around to the back and see if these folks could spare us some food and warmth. Here we are, Wife. I'll knock on the door. 2

Haunt:

Come in! Come in! 3

Narrator:

The family entered, but they didn't see anyone in the house. 4

Wife:

Hello, hello! Is anyone here? 5

Narrator:

No one answered her calls, but because they were all cold and hungry, the husband and wife settled the children down and then looked around a bit. 6

Husband:

Would you look at this? A hot fire with skillets full of food just ready to be cooked and eaten. What do you make of this? 7

Wife:

I don't know, husband, but I am going to take off my wet shoes and stockings and get warm! 8

Husband:

While you're doing that, I think I'll take this pot and fetch some water for coffee. Once you're warm, why don't you just mix up some of that food for our dinner? Maybe some cornbread and beans? 9

From *Scary Readers Theatre.* © 1994 Suzanne I. Barchers. Teacher Ideas Press. P.O. Box 6633, Englewood, CO 80155. 1-800-237-6124.

Wife:
    We might as well. No one is here to tell us differently. Children, warm yourselves by the fire and play a bit while your father fetches some water.

10

Narrator:
    Just after her husband left, a man with no head walked right through the shut door. He had on his britches, shirt, shoes, and coat, but no head. There was only a raw neck and bloody stump. Fortunately, the children were busy playing and didn't see him.

11

Wife: *(Shakily)*
    Who are you? What in the Lord's name do you want?

12

Haunt:
    Other folks have been here, but no one has asked in the Lord's name before. As soon as your husband comes back, I'll tell you who I am and what I want.

13

Narrator:
    About that time, the husband returned and nearly jumped out of his skin with fright. The haunt spoke to them.

14

Haunt:
    Let me tell you what I want you to do. I mostly need you to go with me down into the cellar. There, you must find my head and bury me altogether again.

15

Husband:
    Let me find a torch, and I'll go down with you.

16

Haunt:
    You don't need that.

17

Narrator:
    The headless man stuck his finger in the fire, and his finger blazed up like a torch. The wife told the children to stay by the fire while the haunt led her and her husband down the stairs, lighting a candlestick with his blazing finger.

18

Haunt:
    Now, if you'll dig right here, you'll find my head. And over here, in this hole, is where the rest of me is buried. After that, if you dig over yonder you'll find my barrels of gold and silver.

19

From *Scary Readers Theatre.* © 1994 Suzanne I. Barchers. Teacher Ideas Press. P.O. Box 6633, Englewood, CO 80155. 1-800-237-6124.

Narrator:

So they dug and dug, and when they had the haunt's head on the shovel, he   20
plucked it off and put it on his neck. Then he crawled back into his grave. The
husband and wife dug again until they found the barrels of gold and silver. Then
they heard a voice from below the ground.

Haunt:

You've found my head and joined my corpse together. Now you can have my   21
land, my house, and all my money.

Narrator:

The husband and wife went back upstairs, and seeing that their children were   22
still playing by the fire, washed up and began to cook their dinner. From that
day forward, they lived in that house and had all the food, clothes, and money
they needed. And the headless haunt never bothered them again.

Janet and Tam Lin

SUMMARY

In this tale from Scotland, Janet becomes friends with Tam Lin during her daily walks in the forest. When she discovers he is under a spell, she saves Tam Lin from being sacrificed by the fairy folk on Halloween night.
Reading level: 4.

PRESENTATION SUGGESTIONS

Janet and Tam Lin have the primary roles and should be center stage. The narrator and mother could be at the side, with the mother exiting after her lines.

PROPS

Place Halloween items on the stage: wizard or black witch hats, silhouettes of cats, pumpkins, and so forth. If done in the fall, add corn husks, plants, or murals of trees to indicate a forest.

CHARACTERS

Narrator

Mother

Janet

Tam Lin

Janet and Tam Lin

Narrator:
Janet grew up near a forest in Scotland where people believed the fairy folk lived. Her mother warned her about them.

1

Mother:
Janet, I know you love walking in the forest, but you must always be careful. You know the fairies are about, especially near Halloween.

2

Janet:
Mother, you know I am careful. Besides, there is no other place to gather the berries and flowers that you love.

3

Mother:
Just remember that the fairies can take any shape. Don't trust anyone you meet.

4

Narrator:
Janet listened to her mother, but her love for the forest was strong. One day, she was strolling along when she met a handsome young man.

5

Janet:
Good morning!

6

Tam Lin:
Good morning to you!

7

Janet:
Who are you, and what are you doing in the woods?

8

Tam Lin:
I am Tam Lin, and I am just enjoying the warm sunshine. What brings you down this path?

9

Narrator:
Janet and Tam Lin talked for a while, enjoying each other's company. In spite of her mother's warnings, Janet liked and trusted Tam Lin. Janet came to the woods every day and soon began to care deeply for her young friend.

10

Janet:
Tam Lin, I would like you to come home with me and meet my family.

11

From *Scary Readers Theatre.* © 1994 Suzanne I. Barchers. Teacher Ideas Press. P.O. Box 6633, Englewood, CO 80155. 1-800-237-6124.

Tam Lin:

    Ah, Janet, I can't. I must tell you the truth. When I was a child, I was stolen by the fairy folk. Though I am a mortal and walk the woods by day, the enchantment returns me to their fairyland at night.   12

Janet:

    Oh, Tam Lin, I am sorry. My mother told me about the fairy folk, but I thought it was just a superstition. We'll just continue to meet as before.   13

Narrator:

    One day, Tam Lin looked especially drawn and sad.   14

Janet:

    Tam Lin, what is wrong today? You look so unhappy.   15

Tam Lin:

    Janet, it is time you learn the rest of my story. Every seven years the fairy folks must pay the *teind* to the spirits. They draw their strength from sacrificing a mortal to the spirits on Halloween. This time, I am the one they have chosen.   16

Janet: *(Anguished)*

    Tam Lin, there must be a way to break the spell.   17

Tam Lin:

    There is, but it is very hard. On Halloween night the spell is lifted just long enough for me to leave the forest to go to the circle of stones. If someone who loves me can seize me during the procession and hold me for the time of twenty-one heartbeats, I shall be free of the fairies.   18

Janet:

    Then that is the answer, for I love you enough to break the spell. I will save you!   19

Tam Lin:

    I love you too, but the danger is terrible. The evil spirits are out on Halloween, and you will be at great risk. When you seize me, the fairies will change me into things so horrible you will not be able to hold on to me. I may threaten you and put you in great pain.   20

Janet:

    Don't worry, Tam Lin. I will set you free.   21

Narrator:

The night of Halloween arrived, and most people closed their homes, fearful of 22
the fairy folk and evil spirits. Janet went to the crossroads, hiding and listening
for Tam Lin's approach. Near midnight, she heard someone coming. She saw
Tam Lin, dressed in a white robe, walking between two fairies. As he passed,
she jumped up and threw her arms around him. The fairies changed Tam Lin
into a wolf. He snarled at Janet with drooling fangs.

Janet: *(Loudly)*

It's a trick!
23

Narrator:

Janet held on in spite of her terror, but the wolf changed into a huge, slimy, 24
worm that nearly slithered through her grasp.

Janet: *(Weakly)*

It's just another trick. I must hold on.
25

Narrator:

But the fairies weren't finished. Tam Lin turned into a burning hot statue, but 26
Janet held on. Next, the heat was replaced with a coldness so fierce that her
skin was burned again, but Janet kept holding on. After that, she held a huge
bat that beat its wings, trying to fly away. Janet shut her eyes and continued to
cling to the bat even though she felt her strength slipping away.

Suddenly, the fairies began weeping and screeching. There was a flash of
light, and then it was quiet. Janet opened her eyes and found that she was
holding Tam Lin in her arms.

Tam Lin:

Janet! You've done it! You've broken the spell!
27

Narrator:

Janet was too weak to speak, but she smiled up at Tam Lin. Slowly they walked 28
to Janet's home, and they never returned to the forest.

Rachel's Curse

SUMMARY

In this story from New England, Rachel, an old woman, gives fishermen wise advice about the sea. When two sailors taunt her, refuse to take her advice, and burn her hut, she exacts her deadly revenge.
Reading level: 4.

PRESENTATION SUGGESTIONS

The characters can be arranged across the stage in the order of their parts.

PROPS

Presenters can build on the theme of the sea, including ropes, shells, plastic fish, fishing poles, sailor hats, an anchor, and so forth. Rachel might be dressed in old clothes.

CHARACTERS

Narrator

Fisherman

Rachel

First Sailor

Second Sailor

Rachel's Curse

Narrator:
Rachel lived in a falling-down hut in a small harbor village in Massachusetts. 1
She was old and poor and dressed in rags. But she knew the sea better than any
sailor, and wise people would consult her before taking to the seas.

Fisherman:
Rachel, tell me when I should depart for the best catch. 2

Rachel:
Three days after the full moon. 3

Fisherman:
Thank you, Rachel. Your advice is always appreciated. 4

Narrator:
The fishermen gave Rachel a fish or two in thanks and always heeded her 5
advice. But one day, a ship full of strange sailors came into the harbor. The
sailors came into town to party, and there they heard about Rachel.

First Sailor:
This is but a story of foolishness. No woman can tell us when the seas are right for sailing. 6

Second Sailor:
That's right, only a man can do that. 7

Fisherman:
Don't believe us if you won't, but in this town, Rachel has never told us wrong. 8

First Sailor:
Well, we'll just have to see about that. Let's go find this woman. 9

Narrator:
The two sailors went to see Rachel. 10

First Sailor:
We hear you know everything about the seas, old woman. 11

Second Sailor:
So to prove it, we want you to tell us when it is safe to leave the harbor. 12

From *Scary Readers Theatre*. © 1994 Suzanne I. Barchers. Teacher Ideas Press. P.O. Box 6633, Englewood, CO 80155. 1-800-237-6124.

Rachel:
You probably aren't wise enough to listen, but you should delay your sailing until three days hence.

13

First Sailor:
And why would we do that? What makes you such an expert?

14

Rachel:
I knew the likes of you wouldn't listen.

15

Second Sailor:
Why should we? You're just an ugly hag. You have everyone in this village fooled, but you don't fool us, old crone.

16

Rachel:
You'll live to regret those words. You're a pair of fools. Get out of my sight.

17

Narrator:
The two sailors left, but after a night of partying they decided to teach the old woman a lesson.

18

First Sailor:
Listen, my friend, our ship is going to sail in a few hours. Let's go back to that old hag's hovel and burn it down. That will teach her to call us fools.

19

Narrator:
The sailors sneaked up to Rachel's hut and set it ablaze. The townspeople rushed to put out the fire but couldn't save the hut. They looked for Rachel but couldn't find her until they heard her screaming as the ship made ready to leave the harbor.

20

Rachel: (Loudly)
You should have listened to me! You *are* fools!

21

Narrator:
The townspeople saw Rachel sitting on a rock, but before they could go to her, they saw the ship hit the reef and begin to sink. They rushed down to the harbor to help and were able to save all except the two sailors who had taunted Rachel.

After the bodies washed ashore, the townspeople returned to where Rachel sat on the rock. But when they got there, they found she was dead. They buried her where her hut had once stood. Ever since, the reef has been known as Rachel's Curse.

22

From *Scary Readers Theatre.* © 1994 Suzanne I. Barchers. Teacher Ideas Press. P.O. Box 6633, Englewood, CO 80155. 1-800-237-6124.

The Red Ribbon

SUMMARY

In this popular story, a gentleman wonders why his wife refuses to remove her red ribbon until her dying day.

Reading level: 4.

PRESENTATION SUGGESTIONS

The narrator should stand to the side, with the gentleman and lady in the center.

PROPS

The lady could wear a white dress and tie a red ribbon around her neck. The gentleman could be dressed in a suit. A mural of a cemetery could be the background.

CHARACTERS

Narrator

Gentleman

Lady

From *Scary Readers Theatre.* © 1994 Suzanne I. Barchers. Teacher Ideas Press. P.O. Box 6633, Englewood, CO 80155. 1-800-237-6124.

The Red Ribbon

Narrator:
Once there was a rich young gentleman who was out for a walk on a fine spring day. As he walked by the cemetery, he noticed a pretty lady in a white dress with a red velvet ribbon around her neck.

1

Gentleman:
Good morning, young lady.

2

Lady:
Good morning, kind sir.

3

Gentleman:
I was admiring your lovely dress and the striking red ribbon around your neck.

4

Lady:
Thank you, sir. You're most gracious.

5

Gentleman:
Would you care to walk a ways with me?

6

Narrator:
And so the handsome young couple walked along the street, chatting, and becoming acquainted as young people will do. The gentleman found he was quite enchanted with the lady and asked to meet her again.

7

Gentleman:
May I call on you?

8

Lady:
Of course, sir. I would welcome you at any time.

9

Narrator:
The lady wore beautiful clothes every time they met, but she always wore the red velvet ribbon around her neck. Soon, the young gentleman hardly noticed it. He fell deeply in love with her, and they planned a beautiful wedding.

10

Gentleman:
What sort of necklace would you like to wear with your wedding gown?

11

From *Scary Readers Theatre*. © 1994 Suzanne I. Barchers. Teacher Ideas Press. P.O. Box 6633, Englewood, CO 80155. 1-800-237-6124.

Lady:

None, thank you. My red ribbon is quite enough.   12

Gentleman:

But I don't understand. I could buy you any jewels you fancy.   13

Lady:

This ribbon is enough. I can never take it off, and you must never touch it.   14

Narrator:

The wedding was lovely, and the couple settled into married life. A year passed, and they welcomed a new baby. Still, the red ribbon bothered the gentleman.   15

Gentleman:

I know you don't want me to touch your red ribbon, but aren't you afraid the baby will pull on it? Shouldn't you take it off?   16

Lady:

No, my husband. It must stay just as it is.   17

Narrator:

The years passed by quickly, and the couple enjoyed their life together. Finally, they were growing old, and the lady became ill. Her husband called for the doctor, but the doctor told them that she would die soon.   18

Lady:

My dear husband, I know my time is coming to an end. I also know that you have always wondered why I never would take off my red ribbon. It is time for you to know the truth. You may take off my ribbon.   19

Narrator:

The gentleman slowly removed the ribbon. And the lady's head fell off!   20

From *Scary Readers Theatre*. © 1994 Suzanne I. Barchers. Teacher Ideas Press. P.O. Box 6633, Englewood, CO 80155. 1-800-237-6124.

The Robber Bridegroom

SCARIEST!!!

SUMMARY

In this German tale from the Brothers Grimm, a miller agrees to let a rich man marry his daughter. She visits the rich man's house, but discovers he is a robber who plans to kill her. She escapes and plots his capture.
Reading level: 4.

PRESENTATION SUGGSTIONS

The narrator, bridegroom, and bride should be on stage during the entire script. If preferred, the bird, old woman, and robber could enter for their lines.

PROPS

Props could include a bird or bird cage, a barrel, and various household items or furniture.

CHARACTERS

Narrator
Bridegroom
Bride
Bird
Old Woman
Robber

The Robber Bridegroom

Narrator:

There once was a miller who had a beautiful daughter. When she was grown, he decided she should have a rich husband. When a rich man asked for her hand, the miller promised her to him. But whenever the girl thought about her bridegroom, her heart grew cold. In turn, her bridegroom wondered why she was so cool.

1

Bridegroom:

You are soon to be my bride, yet you never come to visit me.

2

Bride: *(Evasively)*

I don't know where you live.

3

Bridegroom:

Well, my house is just a short way through the forest.

4

Narrator:

Though she tried to find an excuse, he insisted she come for a visit.

5

Bridegroom:

Next Sunday is the day then. I have already invited guests. I will strew ashes along the path to guide you along the way.

6

Narrator:

When Sunday arrived, the girl was very uneasy, although she didn't know why. She filled her pockets with peas and lentils, sprinkling them along the path as she walked. When she came to the middle of the forest, she found a dreary house. She walked in, and in a moment she heard a little voice.

7

Bird:

Turn back, turn back thou pretty bride.
Within this house thou must not 'bide,
For here do evil things betide.

8

Narrator:

She looked around and spied a little bird in a cage. Again, it cried out to her.

9

Bird:
> Turn back, turn back thou pretty bride.
> Within this house thou must not 'bide,
> For here do evil things betide.

10

Narrator:
> The girl searched through the house and finally found an old woman sitting in the cellar.

11

Bride:
> I am looking for my bridegroom. Does he live here?

12

Old Woman:
> Oh, dear child, don't you know where you are? You are in a den of thieves. You will be marrying death. See this kettle of water? They will cut you into pieces, cook, and eat you.

13

Bride:
> What should I do? Is there time to run?

14

Old Woman:
> No, child, they will be here soon. Hide behind this barrel and be still as a mouse. When the robbers fall asleep tonight, we will flee. I have waited a long time to escape, and we shall go together.

15

Narrator:
> Soon the robbers returned, bringing another young girl with them. In no time, they had killed her and cut her into pieces. One thief noticed a gold ring on her little finger, so he chopped it off. But the finger flew into the air and landed in the bride's lap.

16

Robber:
> Where is that ring? I can't find it anywhere. Here, fellows, come and search with me.

17

Old Woman:
> Come now, time for supper. You can find it tomorrow. It's not going anywhere.

18

From *Scary Readers Theatre.* © 1994 Suzanne I. Barchers. Teacher Ideas Press. P.O. Box 6633, Englewood, CO 80155. 1-800-237-6124.

Narrator:

The robbers gave up the search and began to eat. The old woman put a sleeping 19
potion in their wine, and soon they were all snoring loudly. The bride heard
their snores and tiptoed toward the door. The old woman joined her.

Bride:

Look, here is the way back. The peas and lentils have sprouted and are shining 20
in the moonlight.

Narrator:

When the bride and the old woman got home, they told the miller all that had 21
happened. They carefully planned what to do next. Soon it was the wedding
day. The bridegroom and all his friends arrived, and they all sat down for the
feast. Each guest was invited to tell a story.

Bridegroom:

Sweetheart, surely you have a story to share with us.   22

Bride:

Instead of a story, I shall tell you my dream. I was walking through a forest and came 23
to a house. I went in, and it was empty except for a bird in a cage who cried twice:

Turn back, turn back thou pretty bride.
Within this house thou must not 'bide,
For here do evil things betide.

I searched through all the rooms, finding no one except an old woman in
the cellar. I asked her if my bridegroom lived there, and she told me I was in a
den of thieves who would kill me, cut me into pieces, and eat me.
Of course it was a dream, but next the old woman hid me behind a barrel.
The thieves came in, killed a young girl, and cut her into pieces.
Of course it was just a dream, but then one of the robbers saw a ring, and
he chopped off the dead girl's finger to get it. It flew through the air, behind
the barrel, and onto my lap.
And here is the finger with the ring!

Narrator:

She drew out the finger and showed it to the guests. The robber, who had grown 24
deathly white at the girl's story, jumped up to escape. But the other guests held
him and the other robbers. In no time, the authorities arrived, and the thieves
were promptly executed for their crimes.

The Tale of the Talking Eggs

SUMMARY

In this story from American folklore, a young girl's kindness to an old woman is amply rewarded. When her mean sister tries to get the same treasures, her rewards equal her spitefulness.

Reading level: 4.

PRESENTATION SUGGESTIONS

The narrator, old woman, and Little Tater have major roles and should be placed toward the front of the stage. Blossom and Mama can be to the side.

PROPS

Props might include knives, eggs, a bucket, and murals of the forest, heads, or arms. The old woman could be dressed with a shawl over her head.

CHARACTERS

Narrator

Mama

Little Tater

Old Woman

Blossom

From *Scary Readers Theatre.* © 1994 Suzanne I. Barchers. Teacher Ideas Press. P.O. Box 6633, Englewood, CO 80155. 1-800-237-6124.

The Tale of the Talking Eggs

Narrator:

Once there were two little girls born in the spring. One was called Blossom   1
because she was just as pretty as a flower. The other was called Little Tater,
probably because she wasn't as pretty as her sister. Although Blossom was
pretty on the outside, she was mean and spiteful in every other way. But Little
Tater was the sweetest child you could ever hope to meet. Their mama seemed
as blind to Blossom's mean ways as she was to Little Tater's sweetness. And
she sure kept Little Tater busy.

Mama:

Little Tater, take this bucket and go to the well for some water.   2

Little Tater:

Okay, Mama.   3

Narrator:

Even though that bucket was right heavy, Little Tater hummed as she carried   4
it down to the well and filled it up. Suddenly, she heard a voice speaking to her.

Old Woman:

Baby, can you give an old woman a sip of that sweet water?   5

Little Tater:

Yes, ma'am. Come here and help yourself.   6

Old Woman:

Thank you, baby. I'm here.   7

Narrator:

At first Little Tater didn't see anyone, but she felt a cool breeze on her legs.   8
Then she saw an old woman who looked to be at least a hundred years old with
a shawl up over her head. The old woman sipped from the bucket for a long
time.

Old Woman:

Thank you, sweet child. God will bless you.   9

Narrator:

The old woman left, and Little Tater went home with the bucket of water. 10
Although Little Tater was used to being kind to others, her mother always
thought Little Tater was no good. Little Tater never told her about the old
woman, figuring it was of no use. One day, Blossom was so mean to Little Tater,
and her mama so demanding, that Little Tater ran into the woods crying and
rubbing her eyes.

Old Woman:

Don't you be crying, child. Come over here to me. That's it, you just shush your 11
crying. Now let's walk a ways.

Narrator:

They walked into a bramble bush that opened up for them just like it knew they 12
were coming. As they walked, they saw two sharp hunting knives fighting with
each other. Little Tater was amazed but thought it would be impolite to say
anything. As soon as they passed, the knives stopped fighting and fell to the
ground.

Next, they passed two arms fighting just like the knives. Again, Little Tater
tried to ignore them politely. As they passed, the arms stopped fighting and
shook hands with each other.

Next, they came on two heads shouting at each other, and once again, Little
Tater looked politely away. As they passed, the heads stopped fighting, smiled
at each other, and blessed Little Tater.

Old Woman:

Here is my cabin, dear. Would you be kind enough to make a fire? 13

Little Tater:

Of course, ma'am. 14

Narrator:

And then the old woman took off her head, put it in her lap, and began to brush 15
her hair. Little Tater tried not to stare and began to make the fire.

Old Woman:

Here, darling. Take this bone and put it in the pot for dinner. 16

Little Tater:

Yes ma'am. 17

From *Scary Readers Theatre*. © 1994 Suzanne I. Barchers. Teacher Ideas Press. P.O. Box 6633, Englewood, CO 80155. 1-800-237-6124.

Narrator:

Now Little Tater was sorely hungry, but she put that bone in the pot. Soon she smelled a powerful rich stew.

18

Old Woman:

My back surely does itch. Could you scratch it for me?

19

Little Tater:

Yes ma'am. How does this feel?

20

Old Woman:

Ah, that is just fine.

21

Narrator:

When Little Tater finished scratching the old woman's back, she pulled her hand away, and it was all bloody because the woman's back was like broken glass. She tried not to cry but couldn't help herself just a bit.

22

Old Woman:

Here, Little Tater, just let me blow on that hand, and it will be good as new.

23

Little Tater:

Thank you. You're right, it doesn't hurt at all now.

24

Old Woman:

You are a good girl. After we eat, why don't you sleep here tonight? Tomorrow things will be better at home.

25

Narrator:

So Little Tater slept that night, peaceful as a newborn babe. She felt refreshed when she woke the next morning.

26

Old Woman:

Little Tater, you're a fine girl, and here is what I want you to do. Go inside the chicken house. The eggs will be crying out at you, some saying "Take me! Take me!" Now you go ahead and take them. If some say "Don't take me!" you just let them be. Then head on home and throw the eggs over your shoulder, one after the other.

27

Little Tater:

Thank you again, ma'am. You've been most kind to me.

28

Narrator:
Little Tater started home, and as she threw each egg over her shoulder, wonderful treasures appeared: gold, silver, pretty clothes, and even a fine bay horse that carried her home.

29

Little Tater:
Mama, Mama! Come see what I have!

30

Mama:
Where did you get all these things? Tell me now!

31

Little Tater:
Well, once I gave an old woman some water. Yesterday, I saw her in the woods. She took me through the bramble past some fighting knives, fighting arms, and arguing heads right to her cabin. She asked me to help her, then she gave me dinner and some magic eggs that turned into all these treasures.

32

Mama:
Blossom, come here right now! You go find that woman and get some of those eggs!

33

Narrator:
So Blossom found the old woman in the woods, and just as before, the old woman led her through the bramble bush.

34

Blossom:
Look at those knives. How can two knives fight like that? That is just stupid as can be.

35

Narrator:
Those knives just kept on fighting. Next, Blossom laughed aloud at the fighting arms.

36

Blossom:
Now, isn't that the stupidest thing you ever saw? Fighting arms!

37

Narrator:
Those arms kept fighting, and when they passed the shouting heads, Blossom laughed so hard she fell to the ground.

38

From *Scary Readers Theatre.* © 1994 Suzanne I. Barchers. Teacher Ideas Press. P.O. Box 6633, Englewood, CO 80155. 1-800-237-6124.

Blossom:

This is surely the stupidest place I ever saw.   39

Narrator:

As the old woman and Blossom went on, the heads just kept shouting at each   40
other. When they got to the cabin, and the old woman took off her head,
Blossom grabbed it right off her lap.

Blossom: *(Stubbornly)*

Now I ain't giving your head back till you give me all the things you gave my   41
sister.

Old Woman:

You're a shameful girl. God will punish you. But seeing's how I need my head   42
back, here is what you do. Go inside the chicken house. The eggs will be crying
out at you, some saying "Take me! Take me!" Now you go ahead and take them.
If some say "Don't take me!" you just let them be. Then head on home and
throw those eggs over your shoulder, one after the other.

Narrator:

Blossom put the old woman's head on the porch, leaving her inside to grope   43
around without it. In the chicken house, all the eggs were crying out "Take me!"
and "Don't take me!" Blossom just grabbed them all and ran for home.

On the way home, she started tossing them over her shoulder. But instead
of treasures, these eggs were full of snakes, frogs, and tiny whips that snapped
at her head. Instead of a fine horse, an old wolf chased her through the woods
to her mama's house. That wolf was joined by his wicked friends who chased
Blossom and her mama right out of that cabin.

Little Tater, who had been away fetching water at the well, came back to
the empty cabin, with her horse and all her treasures waiting for her. She's been
living in that house ever since, riding that horse and sharing her treasures with
other sweet children. If you go looking, I bet you'll find her still.

Part 4

Aaron Kelly's Bones

Aaron Kelly's Bones

SUMMARY

In this American tale, Aaron Kelly decides he doesn't feel dead and returns to his home, staying until his widow's suitor assists with his return to the grave.
Reading level: 5.

PRESENTATION SUGGESTIONS

This humorous ghost story can be presented with the narrator off to one side, Aaron Kelly in a chair, and the widow in the center. The undertaker and fiddler can enter and exit for their roles.

PROPS

A rocking chair would enhance Aaron Kelly's role. The fiddler could pretend to play a violin. The undertaker could be dressed in dark clothes with a black hat. Additional props such as a rug, a clock, or a table could create a living room setting.

CHARACTERS

Narrator

Aaron Kelly

Widow Kelly

Undertaker

Fiddler

From *Scary Readers Theatre.* © 1994 Suzanne I. Barchers. Teacher Ideas Press. P.O. Box 6633, Englewood, CO 80155. 1-800-237-6124.

Aaron Kelly's Bones

Narrator: *(Somberly)*
Aaron Kelly was dead. His widow bought him a new suit and a fine coffin. After the preacher said some words over him, Aaron Kelly was buried in the grave-yard by the church. But that night, Aaron Kelly climbed out of his coffin and came home. The family was still gathered when Aaron Kelly sat down in the rocking chair by the fire.

1

Aaron Kelly:
What is going on here? Why the long faces? You all look like someone died.

2

Widow Kelly: *(Amazed)*
What are you doing here? You died three days ago. We just buried you.

3

Aaron Kelly:
Don't be daft, old woman. I'm not dead. I feel fine.

4

Widow Kelly:
You may feel fine, but you look dead. Get on back to your coffin in the church graveyard.

5

Aaron Kelly: *(Stubbornly)*
Look, old woman, I'm not climbing back into that coffin until I feel dead.

6

Narrator:
Some days went by, and Aaron Kelly still refused to return to his grave. One evening, the undertaker arrived at Widow Kelly's door.

7

Undertaker:
Widow Kelly, I am sorry to bother you during this difficult time, but you have neglected to pay for Mr. Kelly's coffin.

8

Widow Kelly:
Well, sir, here is the problem. My dearly departed husband won't depart! He refuses to believe that he is indeed dead. I can't collect his life insurance until he stays in his coffin. And until I collect his life insurance, I can't pay you for that coffin.

9

Undertaker: *(Shocked)*
How can this be? We all went to his funeral and saw him put in the ground.

10

From *Scary Readers Theatre.* © 1994 Suzanne I. Barchers. Teacher Ideas Press. P.O. Box 6633, Englewood, CO 80155. 1-800-237-6124.

Widow Kelly:

See for yourself.   11

Narrator:

The undertaker looked at the rocking chair by the fire and saw dead Aaron Kelly   12
sitting there. Every time Aaron Kelly rocked the chair, his bones and joints
squeaked and creaked. The undertaker shook his head in bewilderment and left.

Time passed. The widow went about her affairs, hoping one day her dead
husband would be reasonable and return to his coffin. But dead Aaron Kelly
just sat in the rocking chair by the fire, squeaking and creaking.

One day, a fiddler who wanted to ask the widow to be his wife worked up
his courage and came to court her. While they talked, Aaron Kelly squeaked
and creaked in his rocking chair.

Fiddler:

How long is this going to go on? When will he return to his grave?   13

Widow Kelly:

I don't know what to do. Just ignore him.   14

Aaron Kelly:

You two aren't any fun. Fiddler, why don't you play your fiddle. Let's dance.   15

Narrator:

Not knowing how to say "no" to a dead man, the fiddler began to play. Dead   16
Aaron Kelly creaked his way out of the rocking chair, shook out his old bones,
and began to dance. He tottered about with his leg bones clattering, his teeth
chattering, his kneebones knocking, and his arms rattling. He shook his way
around the room so much that a bone came loose and clattered to the floor.

Fiddler: *(Amazed)*

Looky there!   17

Widow Kelly: *(Insistent)*

Don't stop playing now! Faster!   18

Narrator:

The fiddler played faster, and Aaron Kelly lurched on around the room. Another   19
bone fell to the floor.

Widow Kelly: *(More insistent)*
Keep playing! Faster! Faster!   20

Narrator:
The fiddler played even faster, and those rickety old bones began to rattle to   21
the floor. Soon, all that was left was a pile of bones, except for dead Aaron
Kelly's head. His grinning teeth chattered away while the fiddler played.

Fiddler:
Won't he ever stop? Look at his head!   22

Widow Kelly: *(Even more insistent)*
Don't give up now! Keep playing! Faster! Louder!   23

Narrator:
But the fiddler lost heart for his macabre playing.   24

Fiddler: *(Wearily)*
Widow Kelly, I'm sorry, but I just have to stop this foul fiddling and go home.   25

Narrator:
When the fiddler left, dead Aaron Kelly quieted his chattering. The widow   26
gathered up his bones, and the family helped her take them to his coffin. They
mixed them up right good so that Aaron Kelly would stay dead in his grave.
But the fiddler was not ready to take another chance on marrying Widow Kelly.
She remained a widow until she joined Aaron Kelly in the grave.

The Hydra

SUMMARY

In this Greek myth, Hercules, Athene, and Iolaus go to Lerna to kill the nine-headed Hydra whose poisonous breath is threatening the village. Hercules succeeds with the help of Athene and Iolaus, and the town is safe.
Reading level: 5.

PRESENTATION SUGGESTIONS

The villagers can exit after reading their parts. The narrator can be to the side, with Hercules, Iolaus, and Athene remaining in the center of the stage.

PROPS

Students can make murals of the Hydra, a swamp, or a chariot. Students can also research Greek art and make murals or posters with appropriate accents.

CHARACTERS

Narrator

First Villager

Second Villager

Hercules

Iolaus

Athene

The Hydra

Narrator:
Thousands of years ago, an evil monster lived at the edge of a swamp. This monster was especially fearsome because it had nine heads. The monster's breath was poisonous, bringing death to whoever breathed it. The people in the nearby village of Lerna worried as the deadly mist came closer and closer to their town.

1

First Villager:
Someone must kill the Hydra. If it isn't destroyed, we will have to leave our homes or face death.

2

Second Villager:
I have heard that Hercules is very brave. Perhaps he will be able to kill the Hydra.

3

Narrator:
The villagers sent for Hercules, and soon he and his friend Athene arrived. They were driven in a chariot by Iolaus.

4

Hercules:
Where is this Hydra that I have heard spoken of with such fear?

5

First and Second Villager:
By the swamp!

6

Narrator:
Iolaus drove them out to the edge of the swamp.

7

Iolaus:
There it is! It's beneath the branches of that sycamore tree.

8

Athene:
It looks as though it's sleeping. Perhaps you could go out and kill it before it awakens.

9

Hercules:
But look at the ground. It is too soft to cross, and if the Hydra wakes up, I'll be at a disadvantage.

10

Athene:
Why don't you shoot fire arrows at it? That should wake it, and it will probably come closer so you can kill it.

11

From *Scary Readers Theatre*. © 1994 Suzanne I. Barchers. Teacher Ideas Press. P.O. Box 6633, Englewood, CO 80155. 1-800-237-6124.

Iolaus:

I'll make the fire while you prepare the arrows.   12

Narrator:

Soon Hercules was shooting fiery arrows at the beast. It awoke, and each of its   13
nine heads hissed with anger.

Hercules:

Move back, Athene and Iolaus.   14

Narrator:

Hercules had many swords and spears, but he preferred to use his club. He knew   15
that he would have to kill the beast quickly, because breathing its poison would
kill him. As the Hydra approached, Hercules leaped forward and crushed one
of its heads. But as soon as he smashed one head, another appeared in its place.

Iolaus:

Hercules! Use your sword!   16

Narrator:

But whenever Hercules cut off one of the Hydra's heads, another would grow   17
in its place.

Athene:

Iolaus, help him! Take the fire and burn the beast so it can't grow a new head.   18

Narrator:

So Iolaus took a burning branch from the fire, and each time Hercules cut off   19
a head, he would sear the stump of the neck and the head would die. Soon eight
of the nine heads were destroyed. But when Hercules cut off the ninth head, the
head would not die. It continued to hiss, pouring out its poisonous gas.

Iolaus:

Hercules! Bury the head under this boulder! That should stop it forever.   20

Narrator:

Indeed, burying the head worked, and the evil hissing stopped. Thus was the   21
dreadful Hydra vanquished by Hercules and his friends. The poisonous mist
slowly disappeared, and the people rejoiced at their good fortune.

The Minotaur

SUMMARY

In this Greek myth, fourteen Athenians must be sacrificed to the evil monster, the Minotaur, who lives in a labyrinth on the island of Crete. With the help of Ariadne, Theseus slays the monster, escapes from the maze, and rescues the other victims.

Reading level: 5.

PRESENTATION SUGGESTIONS

All characters could remain on stage throughout the play, with the narrator, Theseus, and Ariadne placed near the front.

PROPS

Students could research Greek art and create murals or pottery with appropriate designs. Other mural ideas include a drawing of a Greek ship, the Minotaur, or a maze.

CHARACTERS

Narrator

Theseus

King Aegeus

Ariadne

King Minos

The Minotaur

Narrator:

Long ago, the people of Crete defeated the people of Athens in a bloody and bitter war. The king of Crete ordered a yearly sacrifice of seven young men and seven young women from Athens to the horrible monster, the Minotaur. This fierce creature was half man and half bull, and it was kept in a labyrinth or maze with winding passageways and only one entrance. For the annual sacrifice, the fourteen young people would be left in the labyrinth to wander through the maze until the Minotaur found and devoured each one. No one had ever found the way out and escaped. 1

The king of Athens had a son, Theseus, who had been away on many adventures. When Theseus returned to Athens, many people rejoiced, but the parents of the next fourteen victims wept with sadness.

Theseus:

Father, why are those people grieving? 2

King Aegeus:

They are the parents of the fourteen who will be sacrificed to the Minotaur. 3

Theseus:

Father, I am going to take the place of one of the young men. I shall be one of those sent to Crete for the sacrifice. 4

King Aegeus:

But son, I can't let you do that. You will be going to your death. 5

Theseus:

I shall not die, but shall kill the Minotaur and end this terrible ritual. 6

King Aegeus:

Son, I admire your courage, but you may not be able to kill this evil beast. And if you do succeed, how will you escape from the labyrinth? 7

Theseus:

There must be a way, father, and I will have the gods on my side. 8

From *Scary Readers Theatre*. © 1994 Suzanne I. Barchers. Teacher Ideas Press. P.O. Box 6633, Englewood, CO 80155. 1-800-237-6124.

Narrator:

The king's heart was heavy, but he saw he could not dissuade his son. The next day, Theseus was on the ship with the thirteen other young people bound for Crete. When they arrived, the cruel King Minos of Crete was waiting for them, accompanied by many soldiers and his daughter, Ariadne. She looked sad as she watched the young Athenians come off the ship, and when she saw Theseus she stared at him with great curiosity.

9

Ariadne:

Father, who is that last young man?

10

King Minos:

They say he is Theseus, King Aegeus' son. He foolishly insisted on taking another man's place.

11

Narrator:

That night when it was dark, Ariadne slipped out of her room and found Theseus resting in the dungeon.

12

Ariadne:

Theseus, listen to me. I cannot bear to think of another sacrifice. I have come to help you and the others escape.

13

Theseus:

Thank you, princess, but I can't run away now. I have come to kill the Minotaur, so no one will ever be sacrificed again.

14

Ariadne:

But the Minotaur is huge and fierce. How will you slay it?

15

Theseus:

That is not my worry. I have this knife. It is the labyrinth I fear. I don't know how I'll escape from the maze.

16

Ariadne:

I can help you with that! I will bring you a sword and some yarn. When you enter the labyrinth fasten the yarn near the entrance. Unwind it as you go through the maze, and when you have slain the Minotaur simply follow the yarn back out again.

17

Theseus:
    Then let us go tonight so no one will be at risk again.   18

Narrator:
    Theseus and Ariadne slipped out of the dungeon, collected the sword and yarn,   19
and crept to the labyrinth.

Theseus:
    Wait here for me. I will slay the Minotaur, return to you, and then we shall free   20
the others. Then we can take the ship back to Athens. Your father will be very
angry with you. Will you come back to Athens with me?

Ariadne:
    I will, Theseus. Please be careful.   21

Narrator:
    Theseus tied the yarn around a heavy rock and entered the labyrinth. As he came   22
to each new passageway, he decided which way to go, unwinding the yarn as
he went. He passed through cobwebs, heard scurrying rats, and once passed a
huge pile of human bones. But he thought about all who had died before and
who would die again if he failed, and he kept going.

    Just as his ball of yarn ran out, Theseus heard heavy footsteps and ragged
breathing. Then, he saw the gleaming red eyes of the Minotaur. The creature
lowered its huge bull's head and roared in anticipation of its next meal. The
Minotaur didn't expect that this victim would pull out a knife, and it bellowed
in shock as Theseus plunged it into a red eye. Then, Theseus drew his sword
and cut off the beast's head.

    Meanwhile, Ariadne heard sounds of the battle and prayed that Theseus
would defeat the Minotaur. Soon, she heard footsteps approaching.

Ariadne:
    Theseus, is that you?   23

Theseus:
    Yes, Ariadne, I have slain the Minotaur. Let us go release the others and return   24
to Athens. Because of your help, no one will ever fear the Minotaur again.

Narrator:
    Thus, the Athenians escaped from Crete, and thanks to Theseus's bravery and   25
Ariadne's help, no one was sacrificed ever again to the monster.

From *Scary Readers Theatre*. © 1994 Suzanne I. Barchers. Teacher Ideas Press. P.O. Box 6633, Englewood, CO 80155. 1-800-237-6124.

The Punishment

SUMMARY

In this tale from India, a holy man is spurned by a princess. He is determined to kill her, but she is rescued by a prince who exacts his revenge on the holy man.
Reading level: 5.

PRESENTATION SUGGESTIONS

The narrator has a major role and should be near the front of the stage. The other characters could be arranged across the stage, remaining onstage throughout the presentation.

PROPS

Because this is an Indian tale, perhaps students could collect brass, incense burners, or holy symbols. A stuffed toy monkey or barrel also could be placed onstage.

CHARACTERS

Narrator
Rajah
Holy Man
Princess
Prince

The Punishment

Narrator:
Once upon a time, a holy man came to the city where he fasted for many days. 1
The rajah came to receive the holy man's blessing and decided he wanted to
keep him all to himself. He built a room and courtyard, invited the holy man to
live there, and allowed no one except those he chose to visit the holy man.

Now the rajah had a daughter whom he had long ago promised in marriage
to another rajah's son. The princess, who was closely guarded, was curious
about the holy man whom she had heard much about. One day, she contrived
to slip away to meet the holy man, and when she came to his hut he instantly
fell in love with her. When the princess saw the love in the holy man's eyes,
she became frightened and ran out of his courtyard. The holy man ran after her.
When she wouldn't stop, he threw his lance at her, wounding her in the leg.
The princess pulled out the lance, limped back to her room, and secretly bound
up her leg, knowing her father would be angry at her for sneaking off to see the
holy man. The next day, the rajah went to see the holy man.

Rajah:
You are quiet today, holy man. Why won't you speak to me? 2

Holy Man:
I have nothing to say that you would care to hear today. 3

Rajah:
Why? Surely you know that I listen to all that you say. Please talk to me. 4

Holy Man:
All right, then. Let me tell you that there is someone, who if not stopped, will 5
kill every person in this place.

Rajah:
What? Who could this be? How will I catch this infidel? Help me plan what to do. 6

Holy Man:
Very well. Here is what you must do. This evil spirit has taken the shape of a 7
beautiful girl, but when I saw it last night, its teeth became horrible fangs, its
eyes glared like coals of fire, and great claws sprang from its fingers.

Rajah:
But if it looks like a beautiful girl, how will I know it? 8

Holy Man:
Search for a girl with a lance wound in her leg. When you have found her, let me know, and I will tell you what to do next.

9

Narrator:
The rajah sent his soldiers throughout the country in search of a girl with a lance wound in her leg. After days of searching, they realized that the only person with such a wound was the princess. The rajah was very disturbed when he went to see the holy man.

10

Rajah:
There must be a mistake. The only person with a lance wound is my daughter.

11

Holy Man:
Ah, but you were deceived. Your daughter was actually stolen at birth, and an evil spirit has taken her place. If you don't listen to me, she will kill you all.

12

Rajah:
This is hard to believe, but I have no choice except to believe what you say. What do I do now?

13

Holy Man:
Send me two carpenters, and I will do the rest.

14

Narrator:
When the carpenters arrived, the holy man had them make a chest that would let in neither water nor air. The rajah brought the princess to the holy man. They shoved her into the chest, nailed it shut, and carried it off to the river where they pushed it into the water. Then the holy man called two of his pupils to come to him.

15

Holy Man:
Listen, my followers. It has been revealed to me that there is a chest floating in the river with something most precious inside. Go down to the stream, watch for it, and bring it to me.

16

Narrator:
The pupils hurried off to the stream, but unbeknownst to them, a prince from a nearby kingdom had noticed this very chest and ordered his men to take it out of the water. As they opened it, the prince's men drew their swords, prepared to defend him from whatever was inside. The princess, nearly dead, revived in the fresh air.

17

From *Scary Readers Theatre*. © 1994 Suzanne I. Barchers. Teacher Ideas Press. P.O. Box 6633, Englewood, CO 80155. 1-800-237-6124.

Princess:

Oh, thank you for saving me! I have had the most dreadful time, nearly fainting 18
from lack of air.

Prince:

Who are you? What are you doing in this chest? 19

Princess:

I am the rajah's daughter. He and the holy man put me into this chest and sent 20
me to my death. And who are you?

Prince:

I am the prince of Dilaram, and you, my dear, were betrothed to me when we 21
were children.

Narrator:

The young people were amazed to meet each other in such an unusual way, and 22
they found they had much to talk about. They went to the prince's palace where
his father welcomed them and ordered a feast in celebration. Later, the princess
decided to tell the prince everything that had happened to her.

Princess:

My friend, there is more to my story. I had heard so much about this holy man 23
that I sneaked out to see him. I could tell that he was enchanted with me, so I
ran away from him. I think that is why he tricked my father into putting me in
the chest. I don't know what fate he had in mind for me.

Narrator:

The prince decided to punish this holy man and called one of his men to him. 24

Prince:

I want you to take the chest in which we found the princess, put the biggest and 25
fiercest monkey you can find in it, and put it back in the river.

Narrator:

Meanwhile, the holy man's followers were still watching for the chest, wonder- 26
ing if it would ever appear. When they finally spotted it, they were very excited
that their leader's vision had been realized. They swiftly carried the chest back
to the holy man's room, where he had been waiting impatiently, anxious to kill
the princess.

Holy Man:

At last, you have brought me the chest. Now I want you to leave me alone with   27
it, and no matter what you hear, do not disturb me.

Narrator:

The followers left, shutting the door. Shortly, they heard the holy man calling   28
for help, but they heeded his directions and stayed outside. The holy man
continued to scream for help, but though they looked at each other in fear and
wonderment, the followers remained outside as they had been bidden. Soon, it
was quiet and they decided to see if the holy man was all right. When they
opened the door, a huge monkey leaped through the doorway and ran into the
fields. Then they saw the holy man's body torn to pieces. When the princess
heard the story, she knew her enemy was dead and made peace with her father.

From *Scary Readers Theatre.* © 1994 Suzanne I. Barchers. Teacher Ideas Press. P.O. Box 6633, Englewood, CO 80155. 1-800-237-6124.

The Thief and the Liar

SUMMARY

In this tale of danger and intrigue, a thief and a liar outwit three kings to make their fortunes. When the liar later discovers that the thief cheated him, the liar tries to collect his missing florins. In an unpredictable ending, the thief and liar once again collaborate and outwit their foes.
Reading level: 5.

PRESENTATION SUGGESTIONS

Because there are many characters, the kings and servants could exit after their lines. The narrator, thief, and liar should keep center stage, with the wife and robber perhaps entering for their lines later.

PROPS

Appropriate props include a branch, a cauliflower head, an egg, gold coins, an ax, a statue, and a coffin made of a box.

CHARACTERS

Narrator

Thief

Liar

First King

First Servant

Second King

Second Servant

Third King

Third Servant

Wife

Robber

The Thief and the Liar

Narrator:

Once upon a time, an out-of-work thief was wandering along the seashore. He passed a man who was looking at the waves.

1

Thief:

I wonder if you have ever seen a stone swimming?

2

Liar:

Of course I have. Not only that, I have seen a stone jump out of the water and fly through the air.

3

Thief:

What an amazing tale! I tell you what, my lying friend. If we become partners we will surely make our fortunes. Let us go to the king's palace in the next country. When we get there, I will gain his ear and tell him the most outrageous lie I can invent. Then you meet with him and support my falsehood, claiming it as truth.

4

Liar:

What a capital plan! Let's be off.

5

Narrator:

The two men set off down the road, and after several days they arrived at the palace. The thief gained his interview with the king and asked for a glass of beer.

6

First King:

I am most sorry, but this year our crops have failed, and we have neither beer nor wine in the whole kingdom.

7

Thief:

That is amazing! I just came from a country where the crops were so rich I saw twelve barrels of beer made out of one branch of hops.

8

First King:

That is impossible. In fact, I'll bet you three hundred florins that this is not true.

9

Thief:

Well, I will bet you three hundred florins that it *is* true.

10

From *Scary Readers Theatre*. © 1994 Suzanne I. Barchers. Teacher Ideas Press. P.O. Box 6633, Englewood, CO 80155. 1-800-237-6124.

Narrator:

The king said he would send a servant to the country to see if the story was true. On the way, the servant met a man who was from that very country.   11

First Servant:

Tell me, then. Is it true that in your country you have vast quantities of hops?   12

Liar:

Indeed, that is the truth.   13

First Servant:

Then tell me how high the hops grow in your country and how many barrels of beer can be brewed from one branch.   14

Liar:

I can't tell you that, but I know that it takes three men with axes three days to cut down one branch.   15

Narrator:

The servant decided he had all the information he needed and wouldn't bother journeying to this distant country. He gave the man ten florins and asked him to repeat this information to the king. The man agreed, and they returned to the palace.   16

First King:

Tell me, what have you learned? Is it true about the hops in that country?   17

First Servant:

Yes it is, your highness. And here is a man from that country who can confirm the truth.   18

First King:

Then I have no choice but to pay my bet.   19

Narrator:

After the king paid the thief the three hundred florins, the partners set out again for another adventure.   20

Thief:

I think I will go to another king and tell him something even more amazing. Once again, be ready to back me up and we shall be the richer for it.   21

From *Scary Readers Theatre*. © 1994 Suzanne I. Barchers. Teacher Ideas Press. P.O. Box 6633, Englewood, CO 80155. 1-800-237-6124.

Narrator:
  In the next kingdom, the thief presented himself to the king and asked for a cauliflower. 22

Second King:
  Ah, I am very sorry. You see, we have had a blight here and all the vegetables have died. 23

Thief:
  That is indeed tragic, for I come from a country where one head of cauliflower filled twelve water tubs. 24

Second King:
  But that is impossible! I can't believe this tale! 25

Thief:
  I will bet you six hundred florins that it is true. 26

Second King:
  And I will bet you six hundred florins that it is not true. 27

Narrator:
  The second king sent for a servant to go to the country and determine the truth of the matter. On his way, the servant met a man who was coming from that very country. 28

Second Servant:
  Tell me, my friend, how large do the cauliflower grow in your country? Can one head fill twelve water tubs? 29

Liar:
  I don't know about that, but once, going to market, I saw twelve horses pulling twelve wagons that held one head of cauliflower. 30

Second Servant:
  Here are ten florins for you if you will come and tell the king what you saw. This saves me a lengthy journey! 31

From *Scary Readers Theatre*. © 1994 Suzanne I. Barchers. Teacher Ideas Press. P.O. Box 6633, Englewood, CO 80155. 1-800-237-6124.

Narrator:

And thus, they returned to the king, who listened to the story and paid the thief   32
the promised six hundred florins. The partners returned to their travels with
nine hundred florins in their pockets. In the next kingdom, the thief once again
sought an audience with the king.

Thief:

Your highness, did you know that in another kingdom there is a town with a   33
church steeple that is the highest of any ever seen? In fact, there is a bird that perches
on that steeple, and its beak is so long it pecks the stars right out of the sky.

Third King:

I don't believe you. That is quite impossible.   34

Thief:

Well, it is quite true, and I will bet you twelve hundred florins that it is true.   35

Narrator:

The third king sent a servant to find out the truth. The servant came upon a man   36
from that very country and stopped him for a moment.

Third Servant:

Tell me, my friend. I have heard that in your country there is a town with a   37
steeple very high and a bird that sits on it and plucks stars from the sky.

Liar:

Well, I don't think I have seen that bird, but once I saw twelve men with twelve   38
brooms pushing a huge egg into a cellar.

Third Servant:

That is amazing! Could you return with me to the king to tell him your story?   39
There's ten florins in it for you.

Narrator:

Once the king heard about the giant egg, he had to pay the thief the twelve hundred   40
florins. Once again, the partners set out, planning to share their gains equally.

The partners decided they had made their fortunes and split the money, separated,
and went their own ways. But unbeknownst to the liar, the thief kept back three of
the liar's florins. Eventually, they each married and settled down with their wives.
One day, however, the liar was counting his florins and realized that the thief had
cheated him. He found the thief's home and demanded his missing florins.

From *Scary Readers Theatre.* © 1994 Suzanne I. Barchers. Teacher Ideas Press. P.O. Box 6633, Englewood, CO 80155. 1-800-237-6124.

Thief:

Come next Saturday, and I will give them to you.   41

Narrator:

Of course the thief had no plans to give up the florins. Instead, when Saturday   42
came, he stretched out on the bed and told his wife to say he was dead. His wife
rubbed her eyes with onion and went to the door when the liar knocked.

Wife:

I am sorry you came all this way, but my husband is dead. I can't pay you the   43
three florins.

Liar:

Well, in that case, I will take my pay with three lashes of the whip.   44

Narrator:

The thief jumped up from his bed, came to the door, said he was miraculously   45
better, and promised to pay the liar the next Saturday. But the next week, the
thief hid under some hay in the hayloft. The wife met the liar at the door.

Wife:

I am sorry you have come again, but my husband is dead.   46

Liar:

Where have you buried him then?   47

Wife:

In the hayloft.   48

Liar:

Then I will take some hay in return for my debt.   49

Narrator:

So the liar took the pitchfork and began thrusting it into the hay. The thief,   50
fearing for his life, crept out and promised he would pay his partner the
following Saturday.

The next week, the thief went to the crypt of the nearby chapel and stretched
himself out on an old stone coffin. But his partner guessed his plan and went to the
crypt himself. When the liar entered the dark crypt, he couldn't see in the sudden
darkness, but he could hear some robbers whispering at the grated windows.

Robber:

> Listen, my fellow thieves. Let us take the bars from these windows, leave our treasure in the crypt, and return for it when we are done with our next adventure. 51

Narrator:

> Fearing discovery, the liar wound his scarf around himself and stood like a statue in a niche in the wall. The robbers entered through the window and began to divide their treasure. There were twelve of them, but in the dim light the leader miscounted and made thirteen piles of gold. He realized his mistake, but their time was growing short. 52

Robber:

> We have an extra pile of gold, but instead of counting it out again, let's have a bit of sport. Whoever can cut off the head of that old stone statue with one stroke shall have the gold. 53

Narrator:

> And with that he took an ax and approached the liar. Just then he heard a ghostly voice. 54

Thief:

> Leave now! If you don't, the dead will arise from their coffins, the statues will come down from the walls, and you will soon be dead. 55

Narrator:

> Then the thief jumped out of his coffin, and the liar jumped down from the niche. The robbers were so terrified, they ran helter-skelter from the crypt, leaving their gold behind. The partners divided the gold between them, and no one, not even the robbers, ever returned to the crypt again . . . alive, that is. 56

Alphabetical Index to Tales

About the Author

Suzanne I. Barchers received her bachelor of science degree in elementary education from Eastern Illinois University, Charleston; her master's degree in education in reading from Oregon State University, Corvallis; and her doctorate of education from the University of Colorado, Boulder.

Formerly a teacher, administrator, and editor, Suzanne continues to write educational resource and textbooks, writes for *Learning* magazine, and teaches graduate classes at the University of Colorado, Denver.

Suzanne is the author of *Creating and Managing the Literate Classroom* (Teacher Ideas Press, 1990), *Wise Women: Folk and Fairy Tales from around the World* (Libraries Unlimited, 1990), *Cooking Up U.S. History: Recipes and Research to Share with Children* (with Patricia C. Marden, Teacher Ideas Press, 1991), *Readers Theatre for Beginning Readers* (Teacher Ideas Press, 1993), *Cooking Up World History: Multicultural Recipes and Resources* (with Patricia C. Marden, Teacher Ideas Press, 1994), and *Teaching Language Arts: An Integrated Approach* (West Educational Publishing, 1994).